FIRST PASSAGE

FIRST PASSAGE

An Introduction to Christian Beliefs

HANS HESS

Address all personal correspondence to:
Hans Hess
P.O. Box 1473
Elizabeth City, NC 27906
www.folec.net

Individuals and church groups may order books from the author directly, or from the publisher. Retailers and wholesalers should consult the Deeper Revelation Books website for a list of our distributors, as well as an online catalog of all our books.

Published by:
Deeper Revelation Books
Revealing "the deep things of God" (1 Cor. 2:10)
P.O. Box 4260
Cleveland, TN 37320
423-478-2843
Website: www.deeperrevelationbooks.org
Email: info@deeperrevelationbooks.org

Deeper Revelation Books assists Christian authors in publishing and distributing their books. Final responsibility for design, content, permissions, editorial accuracy, and doctrinal views, either expressed or implied, belongs to the author.

—TABLE OF CONTENTS—

Acknowledgements

I would be remiss if I did not thank a few individuals here who have made this work possible. First of all, I would like to thank my wife Jackie. It is because of her constant support and encouragement that I have been able to accomplish many things in life, including this work. I also want to thank Sarah and Alex, who have seen their dad spend many hours in church work, study and traveling. Their commitment to God and laughter makes life worth living. Thanks to my mom and dad who initially pushed me toward education and constantly told me that I could do anything I set my mind to. Thanks to my mother-in-law who epitomizes the word encouragement. Thanks to Mike Shreve for his professionalism, character, and patience in working with me to see this work through. Thanks to Bobby Jo Hamilton for the excellent editorial work. And thanks to Tiffany Harris for reviewing this work and Kristina Granstaff for the illustrations. Thanks to Fountain of Life Church where I pastor. The church has made this project possible. And finally, thanks be to God who gives us life and salvation and for whom I write and live.

Hans Hess
Elizabeth City, NC

PUTTING THE PIECES TOGETHER

A passage is defined as a "way of exit or entrance: a road, path, channel, or course by which something passes . . . [or] a corridor or lobby giving access to the different rooms or parts of a building or apartment." A passage can also be more active, "the action or process of passing from one place, condition, or stage to another." Yet an even more appropriate definition may be, "a continuous movement or flow."[1] Entering the Christian life is a passage. It is an entrance into a new way of life. It is an action where you pass from one place to another. In Christ you pass from an old life to a new one.

The greatest decision you ever made was to commit your life to the Lord Jesus Christ. Recognizing this is a great step, a passage so to speak. This book is designed to guide you through the first passage of basic beliefs of Christianity. Christianity is a vast and beautiful faith. This work seeks to piece together the truths of Christianity in a systematic way to help you better understand the faith.

As you first come to know Christ, and as you are initially introduced to the Kingdom of God, there are a lot of pieces that you must put together. There are pieces of doctrine, there are pieces of discipline, and there are pieces of experience. It is my hope that this book will help you put the pieces together and construct a uniform picture of the pathway of Christianity.

In this short work I deal with the most crucial issues integral to establishing you in the faith as a strong, committed Christian. I feel that if you immerse yourself in the study of Scripture, commit to a Bible-believing and Spirit-filled local church, pray and live your life as God instructs, you will be on your way to becoming a strong believer. I have provided this work to you as a pastor of a local church and as one who travels quite frequently preaching revivals and seminars. I feel that the following subjects will assist you in further establishing your Christian root system, so to speak. If it helps you in any way, my work will not be in vain.

Endnotes

[1] http://www.merriam-webster.com/dictionary/passage. Accessed 2013

chapter 1

WHY CHRISTIANITY?

Either Jesus is true and all other religions are false, or other religions are true and Jesus is false. There are no other options.

—Matt Slick[2]

In this world there always seems to be a struggle for power. Whether it is a struggle between political parties, differing factions in a business, or two children playing in the streets, the struggle persists. "Power tends to corrupt; absolute power corrupts absolutely"—this was a phrase, reportedly used by Lord Acton, British historian, to describe the principle that the increase of power tends to lessen a person's sense of morality.[3] This is why we love a person who has access to power but does not use it for his own selfish whims or to boost his ego. We love a person who uses his influence and power to help those who have little or none. In contrast, the world despises a person who wields power and control to the detriment of those under him. A person who uses his power for good has some sort of understanding of those in need. Politicians must visit the areas where a storm has devastated properties and lives to know how to respond properly. A general must visit the battlefield where his soldiers are fighting. A business owner must visit the places where his employees work—that is, if these leaders want to stay in touch with those whom they are leading, the wall of misunderstanding and distance must be broken down.

As we enter into a conversation about Christianity, we must realize there are parallels to the aforementioned concepts. As human beings, we have a difficult time grasping the idea of God. There is a wall of misunderstanding and distance between God and humanity. How can someone that powerful be real? Or, if He is real, how can He empathize with us in our current state? Some have suggested that mankind has to believe in some supreme "Being" to satisfy our questions and perplexities about life. In other words, life makes no sense without God, so man devised the idea of God by the power of his imagination. The French humanist, Voltaire, said, "If God did not exist, it would be necessary to invent him."[4] But this explanation does not really satisfy our hearts or our minds. Something within us longs to reach beyond the skepticism of Voltaire and asks, "Does life have meaning and value without the existence of a 'higher Power'?"

Christianity declares that God does exist and that He has not been silent. In fact, He has spoken to His creation in many ways and at various times. He has breached the walls of misunderstanding and distance. He has visited His people. He has walked in our shoes. Though He possesses all power, He has only used it for good because that is all He is capable of.

The nineteenth-century Danish philosopher and theologian, Søren Kierkegaard, asked,

> What good would it do me to be able to explain the meaning of Christianity if it had no deeper significance for me and for my life; what good would it do me if truth stood before me, cold and naked, not caring whether I recognized her or not, and producing in me a shudder of fear rather than a trusting devotion? I certainly do not deny that I still recognize an imperative of understanding and that through it one can work upon men, but it must be taken up into my life, and that is what I now recognize as the most important thing.[5]

In other words, if God exists, He must mean something to us, and He must touch our lives in the everyday.

Kierkegaard constructed a parable to explain how the Creator has come down to us and touched our lives, breaking down the wall of separation between Him and us. He called it "The King and the Maiden."

Suppose there was a king who loved a humble maiden. The king was like no other king. Every statesman trembled before his power. No one dared breathe a word against him, for he had the strength to crush all opponents. And yet this mighty king was melted by love for a humble maiden who lived in a poor village in his kingdom. How could he declare his love for her? In an odd sort of way, his kingliness tied his hands. If he brought her to the palace and crowned her head with jewels and clothed her body in royal robes, she would surely not resist—no one dared resist him. But would she love him?

She would say she loved him, of course, but would she truly? Or would she live with him in fear, nursing a private grief for the life she had left behind? Would she be happy at his side? How could he know for sure? If he rode to her forest cottage in his royal carriage, with an armed escort waving bright banners, that too would overwhelm her. He did not want a cringing subject. He wanted a lover, an equal. He wanted her to forget that he was a king and she a humble maiden and to let shared love cross the gulf between them. For it is only in love that the unequal can be made equal.

The king, convinced he could not elevate the maiden without crushing her freedom, resolved to descend to her. Clothed as a beggar, he approached her cottage with a worn cloak fluttering loose about him. This was not just a disguise—

the king took on a totally new identity—He had renounced his throne to declare his love and to win hers.[6]

Christianity announces that God descended to mankind out of His pure love for them. This love led Him through suffering, torture, and ultimately death. He left His power and majesty behind to become one of us. He did not announce His coming with lightning bolts from heaven. Rather, He came as a human being, humble, poor, and born into a stable made for animals. He was a real human, so He could be *real* to us.

> *That which was from the beginning, which we have heard, which we have seen with our eyes, which we have looked at and our hands have touched—this we proclaim concerning the Word of life.* (1 JOHN 1:1)

Jesus was a real person whom people heard, saw, and touched. We know something is right when a person uses his power to selflessly help others, especially if it is motivated by a burning love. This is what God has done. He is the lover who cloaked Himself as a commoner to win His beloved. God came near to us.

THE COMMON QUEST

Basically every known culture and group of people on earth either has been or is now religious. What I mean by *religious* is the belief in some higher power, a god or gods. If we survey the various cultures on earth, we will find basic religious beliefs that fit into the following categories: *Indigenous Religions, Hinduism, Buddhism, Jainism, Taoism, Confucianism, Shintoism, Judaism, Christianity, Islam, Sikhism,* and *New Religious Movements.*[7] It is often hard, however, to define what religion actually is. For example, one definition states, "Religion is the varied, symbolic expression of, and appropriate response to, that which people deliberately affirm as being of unrestricted value for them."[8] In simpler terms, religion is mankind's quest for power and meaning beyond itself. Religion is common to man because by it, man seeks to answer the common questions of life with which all must wrestle. Let's look at two common issues that all people face.

A Moral Dilemma

Why do human beings have a sense of right and wrong within them? Most have an opinion of "the way things should be." How many times have we heard a friend or relative say, "If I were president . . ."? Or on the job, how many times have we heard a fellow employee opine, "If I were in charge . . ."? We all seem to have an opinion. There is a gnawing struggle within us, a quest for right and wrong. This quest is evidence of man's inner sense of God.

There is a longing for understanding, justice, and the good in every person. Of course, this quest is often clouded and derailed by evil. Nevertheless, people have a longing to comprehend the grander purpose of their existence. There must be more to life than what is seen. Francis Schaeffer defined this problem as "moral necessity." He said that man is a being with "aspirations, including moral motions for which there is no ultimate fulfillment in the universe as it is. Man has been 'kicked up' in the way that he has developed a feeling of moral motions, when in reality these have no meaning in the universe as it is." In other words, man has a sense of what should be, but the world is out of sync with his feelings. The end result is that man is left with a great sense of alienation; he has a sense of morality, but "the universe as it is . . . is completely out of line with what is there."[9]

The moral dilemma appears in every culture. Every people group wrestles with this inner sense of right and wrong. Ravi Zacharias illustrates this by pointing to fairy tales. In every culture and people group there is a sense of wonder in children reflected in the universality of these myths and fables that usually pit a good against an evil.[10] There are elements in fairy tales that go unquestioned because almost everyone accepts that good should prevail and evil should not.

Also, there is a sense of wonder and mystery in fairy tales. In our quest for understanding, we attempt to strip away all mystery and often all wonder. We want cold, hard evidence. Yet, millions of people love to visit Disney Land every year. Why? They love to be in a place that conveys a sense of wonder. In our search for God, we have to stop and take in the wonder of it all. There is something within us that cries out for God. In our quest to answer the question, "Does God exist?" we must keep a sense of marvel and mystery in our minds and realize that we are not caving in to anti-intellectualism to retain a sense of wonder. In fact, many of the truths of the Christian faith are wrapped in mystery.[11]

In short, there is in each human being an inner sense that tells him that something greater exists than he can see. It requires some sense of awe to imagine this. This is one of the greatest proofs that God exists. No one has appropriately explained the problems and dilemmas of mankind, in spite of our incalculable advances in science, technology, and research. Belief in God, according to Christianity, is the answer to the moral dilemma. The longing in man's heart is his longing for a relationship with his Creator. Every human being has a void in his heart that only God can fill.

A World with a Cause

Some other questions to ponder are these: If God doesn't exist, why does the world exist? Why are we here? If God isn't real, then where did all this stuff around us come from? Many have offered a-theistic (meaning that God is excluded from the cause) theories and suggestions, but none have satisfied. The conclusion of an argument that says, "The world was not created by God," is rather depressing. If we accept the claim that there is no God and that the world was not created by God, then the world exists without destiny or meaning. There is no higher purpose for existence. There is no reason to live beyond that of mere survival. There is no encouraging aspect to life. The French existentialist philosopher, Albert Camus, came to this conclusion. After doing so, he said, "There is but one truly serious philosophical problem and that is suicide."[12] In other words, if there is no God, there is no purpose; if there is no purpose, then why live? Why live if God doesn't exist?

In Christianity, God has revealed His plan and destiny for mankind. This world was created with a cause, with a purpose, and by a loving Creator who has given all of Himself for it. The reason evil and suffering exist is because of humanity's rebellion against God's purpose and destiny for the world. If God doesn't exist, then why even ask any question about suffering, social justice, or what is right or wrong? It only makes sense if God does exist. Because God exists, we believe in social justice; we believe in a right and wrong that transcends time and culture.

GOD HAS REVEALED HIMSELF

Not only does God exist; He has chosen to reveal Himself to mankind. This is called *revelation*.

*The wrath of God is being revealed from heaven against all the godlessness and wickedness of men who suppress the truth by their wickedness, **since what may be known about God is plain to them, because God had made it plain to them.*** (ROMANS 1:18-19, EMPHASIS ADDED)

In revealing Himself to mankind, God has chosen three primary means: through nature, through His Son and through His Word.

Through Nature

God has not only revealed Himself in man's nature; He has revealed Himself in the whole of Nature.

*For since the creation of the world God's invisible qualities—His eternal power and divine nature—have been clearly seen, **being understood from what has been made,** so that men are without excuse.* (ROMANS 1:20, EMPHASIS ADDED)

All we have to do is study creation to understand that it had an author, a Creator. Many different aspects of its story seem to stun the greatest minds and turn our minds to a higher power and source. The awesomeness of this grand production—God's inception of heaven and earth and all that is contained therein—can especially be seen in the formation of human beings. There are certain amazing things we can study about man's design and makeup, such as the phenomenal construction of the human eye and the ingenious design of man's DNA. These two aspects alone should leave us worshipfully captivated. Then there is the human brain—awe-striking in its capability to store "twenty million volumes of genetic information," which is "roughly equivalent to the Library of Congress" in its number of volumes.[13] How could one be aware of such evidence and not conclude that this earth had an intelligent designer, a Creator?

The obvious question is, "If God's handiwork is so undeniably evident in creation, then why doesn't everyone serve God?" The apostle Paul answers this question in the next few verses.

> *For although they knew God,* **they neither glorified Him as God nor gave thanks to Him,** *but their thinking became futile and their foolish hearts were darkened. Although they claimed to be wise,* **they became fools** *and exchanged the glory of the immortal God for images made to look like mortal man and birds and animals and reptiles.* **Therefore God gave them over in the sinful desires of their hearts** *to sexual impurity for the degrading of their bodies with one another. They exchanged the truth of God for a lie, and worshiped and served created things rather than the Creator—who is forever praised. Amen.* **Because of this, God gave them over to shameful lusts.** *Even their women exchanged natural relations for unnatural ones. In the same way the men also abandoned natural relations with women and were inflamed with lust for one another. Men committed indecent*

*acts with other men, and received in themselves the due penalty for their perversion. Furthermore, since they did not think it worthwhile to retain the knowledge of God, **He gave them over to a depraved mind**, to do what ought not to be done. They have become filled with every kind of wickedness, evil, greed and depravity. They are full of envy, murder, strife, deceit and malice. They are gossips, slanderers, God-haters, insolent, arrogant and boastful; they invent ways of doing evil; they disobey their parents; they are senseless, faithless, heartless, ruthless. Although they know God's righteous decree that those who do such things deserve death, they not only continue to do these very things but also approve of those who practice them.* (ROMANS 1:21-32, EMPHASIS ADDED)

This passage of Scripture tracks the progression of sin in mankind. Firstly, man refused the glory and revelation of God. Secondly, he exchanged God's glory and revelation for created things and worshipped them. Thirdly, and consequently, the Creator let man run his course, a course that led to the full manifestation of evil and all sorts of lewd behavior. In all of this mix, the glory of God was veiled even more, leaving man even more inclined to refuse believing in the God that he knew was there. It can be justifiably said that a certain kind of spiritual *blindness* occurred.

Paul described this blindness in his first letter to the Corinthians:

And even if our gospel is veiled, it is veiled to those who are perishing. The god of this age has blinded the minds of unbelievers, so that they cannot see the light of the gospel of the glory of Christ, who is the image of God. For we do not preach ourselves, but Jesus Christ as Lord, and ourselves as your servants for Jesus' sake. (2 CORINTHIANS 4:3-5)

With God's glory obscured by man's disobedience, the struggle ensued and does so to this day, as man's inner sense of God and creation's open revelation of Him pit themselves against this blindness to "the light of the gospel of the glory of Christ."

Through His Son

Man's built-in awareness of God and creation's vouching for the same are not God's only ways of revealing Himself. He has made Himself known in human form. Through Jesus, He revealed Himself in the flesh. God appeared in many different ways and on many different occasions in the Old Testament, but it was in the New Testament that He actually revealed Himself as a human being. And as such, it would not be an exaggeration to say that this human being, Jesus, has been the most influential and controversial figure in history of the human race. And why wouldn't He be? He was, after all, far more than a man of history, being declared by the Bible and heralded by Christianity as God in the flesh who came to earth and offered Himself for the sins of humanity. He was the supreme, unable to be improved upon, revelation of God to mankind.

Through His Word

God, however, has given us even further revelation of Himself. Not leaving us to our own devices, He has given us His Word. And this Word, God's truth, has not been left to a select few or to a higher class of individuals. By moving on various people throughout many centuries, this Word has been kept and passed on from generation to generation. Because it has been put in written form in the Bible, its message has been accurately preserved. As well, the written Word has made God's message accessible to many more people than it otherwise would have been.[14]

Christianity declares that the Bible is inspired by God. The Word of God itself declares that it is inspired by God. By *inspiration* we mean that the Scriptures were spoken by God or "God-breathed."

> *All Scripture is God-breathed and is useful for teaching, rebuking, correcting and training in righteousness.* (2 TIMOTHY 3:16)

Jesus also spoke of the inspiration of Scripture. In the following references, He equated "Moses and the Prophets" with one returning from the dead with a message from paradise.

> *Abraham replied, "They have Moses and the Prophets; let them listen to them."*
> *"No, father Abraham," he said, "but if someone from the dead goes to them, they will repent."*
> *He said to him, "If they do not listen to Moses and the Prophets, they will not be convinced even if someone rises from the dead."* (LUKE 16:29-31)

Christianity was built upon the words of the apostles and prophets.

> *[The Church is] built on the foundation of the apostles and prophets, with Christ Jesus Himself as the chief cornerstone.* (EPHESIANS 2:20)

Of significance is a message found in the last book of the Bible—a message that appears as a warning that this book should not be added to or taken away from, that it is a closed, complete word. If anyone tries to add *another revelation* into this book's Scripture, there is assurance that disaster will follow.

> *I warn everyone who hears the words of the prophecy of this book: If anyone adds anything to them, God will add to him the plagues described in this book. And if anyone takes words away from this book of prophecy, God will take away from him his share in the tree of life and in the holy city, which are described in this book.* (REVELATION 22:18-19)

It is quite appropriate that this warning appears in the last chapter of the last book of the Bible, as it could be applied to the rest of the Bible as well. As Christians, we can receive revelation by the Spirit, and God can speak to us, but none of these should take away from the completeness of the Scriptures. In fact, any spiritual insight we receive should be confirmed by Scripture.

The Bible is not only inspired by God, and closed and complete, at that; it is truthful and accurate. We use a term, the term *inerrancy*, to describe the accuracy and authority of God's Word. Milliard J. Erickson gives the following definition of inerrancy: "The Bible, when correctly interpreted in light of the level to which culture and the means of communication had developed at the time it was written, and in view of the purposes for which it was given, is fully truthful in all that it affirms."[15] Basically, this means that God moved upon different individuals to write down His words. However, the transmission of the text throughout the centuries must be taken into consideration. That is why this definition includes the phrase, "at the time it was written." Also, correct interpretation of the text in light of the culture and communication of the times it was written must also be considered. Scripture is God inspired and infallible in its original context and form. Thus, we have a sure guide for our faith. The Word of God leads us, directs us, and advises us into the way of holiness. It is *the* Word of God.

WHAT MAKES CHRISTIANITY UNIQUE?

The next question that needs to be addressed is this: *If God does exist and He is the Creator of the world, what makes Christianity true—because there are many other religions to choose from that could be right?* This is an excellent and legitimate query. Let us look at some comparisons between the major religions.

All religions cannot lead to God if they claim to be conveying truth. Why? Each religion claims different truths—*that's why.* Every religion cannot be right; some have to be wrong—that is, if truth holds any meaning at all.

Christianity Offers a Real Solution to Man's Problem of Sin

Hinduism believes in the existence of many gods. This belief simply does not mesh with Christianity, which declares there is one God. In Hinduism, each person has a divine spark within him, and the quest of life is to uncover the god within. If all of the answers to the human dilemma can be found within, there is no need for help from without. Thus, there is no need for a savior. This is diametrically opposed to Christianity. *Christianity is unique in that it declares that mankind is in desperate need of a savior.*

Christianity is the only religion that offers a solution to human wickedness.[16] Jesus identified the source of man's problems as coming from within.

*For from within, out of men's hearts, come evil
thoughts, sexual immorality, theft, murder, adultery, greed, malice, deceit, lewdness, envy, slan-
der, arrogance and folly. All these evils come from
inside and make a man "unclean."* (MARK 7:21-23)

Jesus made no bones about it—wickedness is a human
condition. But, just as He identified the problem, He also
provided a solution for the problem. Jesus came to take
away the sins of humanity. To all who cling to Him, He
grants forgiveness of sins. Not only that—He also grants
the power to overcome the dominion or rule of sin. Sin
isn't just swept under the rug; it is conquered.

Christianity Declares Evil Has Been Defeated

In primal or indigenous religions, the key to life is main-
taining a spiritual balance with the universe because there
are good and bad spirits that inhabit elements of the world.
The way to maintain a peaceful existence is to appease
these bad spirits and to invoke the expertise of spiritual
mediums to assist with this. This is diametrically opposed
to Christianity. In Christianity, the world is good because
it was created by God. Yes, there are bad spirits (demons)
and there are good spirits (angels). However, through the
work of Christ on the cross, we have power over all the
realm of the demonic. Thus, no balance needs to be pur-
sued. *Christianity is unique in that it declares that Jesus
won the victory over the evil forces in the spirit realm.*

*And having **disarmed the powers and authorities**, He made a public spectacle of them, triumphing over them by the cross.* (COLOSSIANS 2:15, EMPHASIS ADDED)

Christianity Says Jesus Is the Only Way to God

Other eastern religions such as Buddhism and Taoism are not really centered on the worship of God but are focused on properly ordering one's life. To the Taoists, there exists a life force (*chi*), and the goal of life is to maintain a balance or proper flow of the chi power in life. This has given rise to the martial arts and an emphasis on meditation, supposedly to increase the level of the life force flowing through a person. In Buddhism, one is to follow an eight-fold path to end suffering in the world. This path includes right view, intention, speech, action, livelihood, effort, mindfulness, and concentration. Through the practice of these, the person engaged in doing so supposedly reaches a higher level of existence and eventually Nirvana at death. Nirvana was described by one Buddhist scholar as *nothingness*. This also is quite obviously opposed to Christianity, *which is unique in that it declares that there is only one way to achieve peace with God, that way being through faith in Jesus.*

Therefore, since we have been justified through faith, we have peace with God through our Lord Jesus Christ. (ROMANS 5:1)

Christianity States Jesus Was God in the Flesh

Islam was developed around six hundred years after the birth of the Christian church, and there is good evidence that Mohammed (its founder) was initially influenced by certain Nestorian Christians.[17] Mohammed's understanding of Christianity seemed to be skewed, however, in that he received only a sketchy knowledge. Islam accepts certain truths from Judaism and Christianity but changes many things and interprets them through its eyes. It accepts that God is one, yet Mohammed is considered to be the last great prophet. Islam, as well, does not believe that Jesus was divine or that He died on the cross. This, of course, is diametrically opposed to Christianity. Either Islam or Christianity is not correct—*both* cannot be valid, credible religions in which one should invest his faith. The most significant difference between the two is that Islam does not believe that Jesus was the Son of God and that He died for the sins of mankind. There is no savior in Islam. And we are left to consider that if ours is to be a sound and reasonable faith, we cannot say that all religions lead to God *unless* we do not believe in truth.

Christianity, alone, claims that God has provided a sacrifice for the sins of mankind. Christianity, alone, says that salvation is available only through faith in Jesus. Christianity, alone, declares that Jesus will return and judge all mankind and correct the evil and suffering on the earth. Christianity, alone, provides the complete answer to the problem of evil and suffering in the world.

Christianity Offers the Solution to Death

Jesus is the only religious teacher who claims to have died and risen from the dead. Of great importance is the fact that the account of His resurrection is one of the most documented events in ancient history, with the evidence for such being absolutely overwhelming. Not only did Jesus appear after His resurrection to His disciples, who later testified to this in their writings; He also appeared to over five hundred others. Noteworthy also is the observation that something caused the disciples to come out of hiding and become bold witnesses for Jesus after His resurrection and ascension. What would have caused such a turn? A reasonable conclusion would be that they must have been actual witnesses of the living, resurrected Jesus. In addition, right on the heels of its inception, the early church developed traditions that commemorated the Resurrection, such as the practice of the believers meeting on the first day of the week. Why would they do this, when in Jewish tradition the Sabbath was held on the last day of the week? The early Christians changed the day because Jesus resurrected on the first day of the week. Also, baptism—that not only imitated what Jesus had done, but commemorated His death, burial, and resurrection—became a ritual in the early church. Just as Jesus conquered death, all those who follow Him conquer death. When a Christian dies, he awakes in the presence of the Lord. The apostle Paul, in 2 Corinthians

5:8 KJV, substantiates this: "We are confident, I say, and willing rather to be absent from the body, and to be present with the Lord."

The Christian conquers the fear and dread of death in knowing that a better future awaits him. In the end, all of the believers will be resurrected. Believers will follow the example of their Lord in His resurrection. Christianity is the only religion that offers that assurance and surety. Christians know where they are going when they die.

We can conclude that God does exist. However, not only does He exist; He has chosen to reveal Himself through our inner sense, through nature itself, in the person of Jesus, and in the written Word. Christianity stands out as unique among the religions of the world in its claims to truth and in its solitary means of salvation—*faith in Jesus alone.*

Endnotes

[2] Matt Slick, "Why believe in Christianity over all other religions?" [http://carm.org/why-believe-christianity-over-all-other-religions] Accessed September 2012.

[3] This concept seems to fly in the face of the liberation theologies in certain parts of the world. [http://www.bartleby.com/59/13/power-tendsto.html]. Accessed September 2012.

[4] Voltaire quoting himself in his Letter to Prince Frederick William of Prussia (1770-11-28), Voltaire in His Letters, trans. S.G. Tallentyre (Honolulu: University Press of the Pacific, 1919).

[5] Søren Kierkegaard, *The Journals of Søren Kierkegaard*, trans., ed. Alexander Dru (London: Oxford university Press, 1938), 15.

[6] Søren Kierkegaard, *Parables of Kierkegaard*, ed. Thomas Oden (Princeton: Princeton University Press, 1978), 40.

[7] I have chosen these categories and definitions based upon Mary Pat Fisher, *Living Religions* (Upper Saddle River, NJ: Prentice Hall, 2002). Huston Smith has chosen the term "Primal Religions" instead of "Indigenous" (see Huston Smith, *The World's Religions* [San Francisco: Harper, 1991]).

[8] T. William Hall, ed. *Introduction to the Study of Religion* (San Francisco: Harper and Row, 1978), 19.

[9] Francis Schaeffer, *He Is There and He Is Not Silent* (Wheaton: Tyndale, 2001), 21.

[10] Ravi Zacharias, *Can Man Live Without God?* (Waco: Word, 1994), 78.

[11] Some have tried to eliminate the term "God" from public discourse altogether. "What would happen were the word [God] to vanish altogether? Karl Rahner has rightly answered that then we would no longer be confronted by the one totality of reality or the one totality of our own existence. The word 'God,' and that word alone, does this." Wolfhart Pannenberg, *Systematic Theology*, vol. 1 (Grand Rapids: Eerdmans, 1991), 73.

[12] Albert Camus, *The Myth of Sisyphus,* trans. Justin O'Brien (New York: Alfred A. Knopf, Inc.), 1955.

[13] Norman Geisler and Peter Bochino, *Unshakable Foundations: Contemporary Answers to Crucial Questions About the Christian Faith* (Minneapolis: Bethany, 2001), 137.

[14] Wayne Grudem, *Systematic Theology* (Grand Rapids: Zondervan, 1994), 50.

[15] Millard Erickson, *Christian Theology* (Baker: Grand Rapids, 1985), 233-234.

[16] Michael Green, *But Don't All Religions Lead to God?* (Grand Rapids: Baker, 2002), 45.

[17] This refers to a group of churches who follow Nestorius (386-451 A.D.). Nestorius was declared a heretic because of his views of Christ. He was condemned by Cyril of Alexandria, who accused him of making Christ into two different persons—one God and one man. Roger E. Olson, *The Story of Christian Theology: Twenty Centuries of Tradition and Reform* (Downers Grover: IVP, 1999), 211.

chapter 2

JESUS—
The Attracting Point of Christianity

> I am an historian, I am not a believer, but I must confess as a historian that this penniless preacher from Nazareth is irrevocably the very center of history. Jesus Christ is easily the most dominant figure in all history.
>
> —H.G. Wells[18]

It really doesn't make sense to write a book about basic Christian beliefs and not include a chapter about the person at the center of the faith—*Jesus.* Jesus is the centerpiece of the Christian faith. In fact, He is the center of all human history. Furthermore, He is the attractive point of Christianity. When one comes to accept the Christian faith, it is because he is attracted to the life, message, and person of Jesus more so than doctrines, creeds, or rituals.

It is a well-known adage that people often follow a person rather than a movement, party, or government. Just think about the power of influential political leaders throughout history. Whether we mention a good personality or a bad one, the evident concept is that people follow a person who emulates an ideal of the way they think things should be.

Recent attention has been drawn to three public figures in the twentieth century who influenced a major political and societal shift in Eastern Europe—Pope John Paul II, Prime Minister Margaret Thatcher, and President Ronald Reagan. Each of these highly visible people sought to break through the Iron Curtain separating Eastern Europe from the rest of the world. The amazing cross-pollination, and to some extent collaboration, of this dynamic is detailed in John O'Sullivan's book, *The President, the Pope, and the Prime Minister: Three Who Changed the World.*[19] O'Sullivan points out that all three of these figures were unlikely candidates to rise to prominence in their own spheres. Reagan was considered by many to be too old and too conservative. Thatcher was also considered by many to be too conservative, and she was a lady to boot. Karol Wojtyla (Pope John Paul II) was an unlikely pope, being only fifty-six years old, adhering to very conservative Catholic values, and being from a nation under the control of communism, with that nation being Poland. All three of these individuals survived assassination attempts on their lives. All three, apart from their great accomplishments, displayed leadership qualities that transcended national and religious boundaries. Each one inspired people to hope again. Each one was resolute and determined. Yet, the ability of all three to inspire others to a better good is what distinguishes them the most.

Many of us will never forget President Reagan standing in front of the Berlin Wall on June 12, 1987, and saying,

> There is one sign the Soviets can make that would be unmistakable, that would advance dramatically the cause of freedom and peace...Secretary General Gorbachev, if you seek peace—if you seek prosperity for the Soviet Union and Eastern Europe—if you seek liberalization: come here, to this gate. Mr. Gorbachev, open this gate. Mr. Gorbachev, tear down this wall. . . Standing before the Brandenburg Gate, every man is a German, separated from his fellow men. Every man is a Berliner, forced to look upon a scar.[20]

Who can forget Margaret Thatcher's toughness and unwavering leadership during these times? Once she said, "Democratic nations must try to find ways to starve the terrorist and the hijacker of the oxygen of publicity on which they depend."[21] This is still sound advice for today. In addition, this mighty woman inspired people to hope, saying, "I am in politics because of the conflict between good and evil, and I believe that in the end good will triumph."[22]

As equally unforgettable (as President Reagan's and Prime Minister Thatcher's memorable examples of toughness, leadership, and inspiration) was when John Paul II encouraged his brothers and sisters under communist domination to have hope. This pope-to-be had grown up in Poland and witnessed the difficulties of his country's people living under Nazi occupation. He had been through hard times, yet he persevered and became the youngest bishop in Poland at the age of thirty-eight. His election as pope occurred on the heels of the controversial death of Pope John Paul I, who only served thirty-three days as pope before his sudden death. After rising to the papacy, John Paul II encouraged his fellow countrymen in Poland, through speeches and numerous papal visits, to hope and not fear in the midst of their oppression. They responded with a great sense of national pride and hope. Eventually communism was dismantled and the communist regimes of Eastern Europe fell like dominoes in the succeeding years.

There seems to be an instinctive longing within each person to follow someone who brings out the best in him. Maybe it is because each of us actually sees the good that we instinctively know should be present in the world. And, whether we realize it or not, we recognize that something is fundamentally wrong with the world—as in, evil and suffering, terrorism and war. We recognize the presence of evil, but good is there, as well—and we *long* to see the good manifest.

Jesus came as the ultimate expression of good. He was a great teacher, a preacher, a healer, a compassionate person, and a zealous Jew. However, He was not only these *things* (as in, not only did He fulfill these *roles*)—He was *good*. He was good in that He was the *very* manifestation of good. This is not to say that His story is only one of great miracles and triumphs; it is a story of tragedy and death, as well, making Him one who is "touched with the feeling of our infirmities," who "was in all points tempted like as we are" (Heb. 4:15 KJV). But it is this very combination that has made the chronicling of Jesus' life one that has resounded universally and changed the destinies of countless souls.

I have heard accounts of missionaries going to remote villages in countries around the world and showing "The Jesus Film" (a movie of the life of Jesus often using actors from the culture being reached). Often after the local people had seen the unjust execution of Jesus, even if they had never heard of Jesus or the Gospel story before, they stood up and protested. Why? Even though these people had never been exposed to the Gospel before, they knew something was absolutely wrong with killing an innocent man.

THE CENTRAL CLAIM OF CHRISTIANITY

The most pressing question on the problem of faith is whether a man as a civilized being can believe in the divinity of the Son of God, Jesus Christ, for therein rests the whole of our faith.

Fyodor Dostoevsky[23]

The entire message of Christianity rests upon this question—*Who was Jesus?* Or, phrased another way, the question reads: *Was Jesus really who He said He was?* The answer to this question defines all of history. If Jesus was a mere man, then all of Christianity is a farce, a lie at best. If Jesus was the Son of God, God in the flesh, the incarnate deity, then Christianity is true and all other philosophies, religions, and ideas must bow to this truth. The well-known Oxford literature professor, C.S. Lewis, tackled the question of Jesus and developed a unique answer.

Lewis wanted to prevent the argument, "I'm ready to accept Jesus as a great moral teacher, but I don't accept His claim to be God." So, Lewis argued,

> That is the one thing we must not say. A man who was merely a man and said the sort of things Jesus said would not be a great moral teacher. He would either be a lunatic—on the level with the man who says he is a poached egg—or else he would be the Devil of Hell. You must make your choice. Either this man was, and is, the Son of God: or else a madman or something worse. You can shut Him up for a fool, you can spit at Him and kill Him as a demon; or you can fall at His feet and call Him Lord and God. But let us not come with any patronising nonsense about His being a great human teacher. He has not left that open to us. He did not intend to.[24]

If we believe Jesus was a good teacher, then His teachings must have been good. How can something be good if it isn't true? So, if Jesus was a good teacher, His teachings were true. The content of His teachings included His identity. One day, in a dispute with religious leaders, Jesus made a statement that revealed His identity to a hardened, recalcitrant crowd.

> *"You are not yet fifty years old," the Jews said to Him, "and you have seen Abraham!"*
> *"I tell you the truth," Jesus answered, **"before Abraham was born, I am!"***
> *At this, they picked up stones to stone Him, but Jesus hid Himself, slipping away from the temple grounds* (JOHN 8:57-59, EMPHASIS ADDED).

> *"...what about the One whom the Father set apart as His very own and sent into the world? Why then do you accuse Me of blasphemy because I said, "I am God's Son"?* (JOHN 10:36)

The little phrase, "I am," was filled with meaning for the Jews. In the book of Exodus, God told Moses that he should tell the Israelites, "I AM has sent Me to you" (Ex. 3:14). God revealed Himself as the "I AM." In John 10:36, we have just read that Jesus used the same term for Himself.

Jesus also taught that He was the only way to God. There are no alternatives. There are no parallel religious tracks provided for people to get to God.

> *Thomas said to Him, "Lord, we don't know where You are going, so how can we know the way?"*

Jesus answered, "I am the way and the truth and the life. No one comes to the Father except through Me. If you really knew Me, you would know My Father as well. From now on, you do know Him and have seen Him." (JOHN 14:5-7)

The Bible declares that Jesus is the Son of God. At the beginning of his Gospel, John paints a deep theological picture of the pre-existing Son of God,

In the beginning was the Word, and the Word was with God, and the Word was God. He was with God in the beginning. Through Him all things were made; without Him nothing was made that has been made. In Him was life, and that life was the light of men. The light shines in the darkness, but the darkness has not understood it. (JOHN 1:1-5)

Much theological debate and writing have ensued because of John's prologue. Yet, it still stands, a sweeping statement—before time, the Word [Jesus] was with God, and indeed was God. He existed with the Father, as One, in the eternal past. There was never a time when God didn't exist. Thus, there was never a time when Jesus didn't exist.

John goes on to write:

The Word became flesh and made His dwelling among us. We have seen His glory, the glory of the One and Only, who came from the Father, full of grace and truth. (JOHN 1:14)

The real miracle of Christmas, therefore, is that the God of the whole world became human. That Jesus came to earth is the greatest story ever told. He was Immanuel— God *with us*; He was Jesus—*Jehovah is salvation*. John later described Him as the "Alpha and Omega . . . the first and the last" (Rev. 1:8, 11). He was not an ordinary man; He was God.

For the first few centuries of the Christian church, theologians, preachers, and common people tried to understand this mystery and to express it in words. This struggle gave way to theological debates and writings. Finally councils of church leaders were held where the leaders meted out a solution to the problem. You see, the mystery of who Jesus was had several sticky elements. Jesus was a man, a common man. He had emotions, tears, joy, sadness, and the like. Yet, Jesus was God in the flesh— He walked on water; He healed the sick; He calmed the seas with a word; He rose from the dead. How would the church reconcile these two different views of Jesus?

The debate over who Jesus was ultimately coalesced into two basic camps. On one side, people stressed the human-side of Jesus. On the other side, people were concerned with preserving the divinity of Jesus. It is important to understand these two camps because, in many ways, we still see these divergent views of Jesus today. Referring back to the first few centuries of the Christian church, some believed that Jesus was too God to be a *real* person. If He was God, how could God become a person?

Secondly, some believed Jesus was too human to really be God. How could this man be God?[25] Yet, the early church developed a wonderfully balanced view of Jesus, in light of the Scriptures and tradition, and declared,

> We believe in one Lord, Jesus Christ, the only Son of God, eternally begotten of the Father, God from God, Light from Light, **true God from true God,** begotten, not made, of one Being with the Father. Through him all things were made. For us and for our salvation he came down from heaven: by the power of the Holy Spirit he became incarnate from the Virgin Mary, and was made man. For our sake he was crucified under Pontius Pilate; he suffered death and was buried.
>
> On the third day he rose again in accordance with the Scriptures; he ascended into heaven and is seated at the right hand of the Father. He will come again in glory to judge the living and the dead, and his kingdom will have no end.[26]

The central claim of Christianity is that Jesus was God in the flesh. God took upon Himself the form of a man. He lived a perfect, sinless life, and died on the cross for the redemption of mankind.

WHY DID GOD BECOME MAN?

After having established who Jesus was, the next logical question is: *Why did He become man?*[27] He did so because it was necessary. The work that Jesus accomplished could not have been accomplished by any other human, or even an angel. Let's look at the reasons it was necessary for the Son of God to become man.

To Reveal God's Nature to the World

What is God like? All we have to do to answer this question is look at the life of Christ.

If God had a name, what would it be? If He had a face, what would it look like? We are clearly given the answers to these questions in Scripture—*Jesus.*

> *In the past God spoke to our forefathers through the prophets at many times and in various ways, but in these last days He has spoken to us by His Son, whom He appointed heir of all things, and through whom He made the universe. The Son is the radiance of God's glory and **the exact representation of His being**, sustaining all things by His powerful word. After He had provided purification for sins, He sat down at the right hand of the Majesty in heaven.* (HEBREWS 1:1-3, EMPHASIS ADDED)

> **He is the image of the invisible God**, *the firstborn over all creation. For by Him all things were created: things in heaven and on earth, visible and invisible, whether thrones or powers or rulers or authorities; all things were created by Him and for Him. He is before all things, and in Him all things hold together. And He is the head of the body, the church; He is the beginning and the firstborn from among the dead, so that*

in everything He might have the supremacy. **For God was pleased to have all His fullness dwell in Him,** *and through Him to reconcile to Himself all things, whether things on earth or things in heaven, by making peace through His blood, shed on the cross.* (COLOSSIANS 1:15-20, EMPHASIS ADDED)

At one point in His ministry, Jesus told His disciples that He was going away, and He assured them that He would return for them. He also told them, "You know the way to the place where I am going" (John 14:4).

As already shared in our previous discussion regarding Jesus being the only way to God, the disciple Thomas replied, "Lord, we don't know where You are going, so how can we know the way?" (v. 5).

Jesus responded, "I am the way and the truth and the life. No one comes to the Father except through Me. If you really knew Me, you would know My Father as well. From now on, you do know Him and have seen Him" (vv. 6-7).

This puzzled Philip. In response, he requested, "Lord, show us the Father and that will be enough for us" (v. 8).

Jesus then answered, "Don't you know Me, Philip, even after I have been among you such a long time? Anyone who has seen Me has seen the Father. How can you say, 'Show us the Father'?" (v. 9).

Jesus came to reveal God to humanity, and He began with a small group of men whom no one would have considered worthy of this revelation. This is the beauty of the ministry of Jesus. He ministered to those on the fringes of society. He welcomed and ministered to women. He allowed the lepers and diseased to come near Him to be healed. He defied the religious establishment with His radical teaching. He is what God is like.

To Reveal to the World Radical Obedience to God

Jesus not only revealed God to us; He also revealed true humanity to us. As the Son of God, Jesus came to earth through a miraculous birth. Yet, as man, He suffered persecution, felt hunger and thirst, was tempted to sin in every way that you and I are, endured betrayal, and was finally executed in total injustice. He was very much a man.

In His earthly life, Jesus displayed perfect and radical obedience to the will of God. He was the perfect example of a life sold-out to God. He began His ministry by being baptized at the river Jordan by John the Baptist. The heavens opened, the Holy Spirit descended upon Him, and the voice of God spoke from heaven saying, "This is My Son, whom I love; with Him I am well pleased" (Matt. 3:17). In ministering to people, Jesus was remarkable. He could tell what people were thinking before they spoke. He could hear the thoughts of the doubting religious leaders who stood on the sidelines as He ministered to people. He could discern the faith, or lack thereof, in a person's heart. He could foretell His future and the future of His disciples. How? He was the Son of God, yes, but He was also anointed by the Holy Spirit and operated as a person full of God's Spirit. In two different verses Jesus gave an insight into how He ministered. First of all, He ministered through the power of the Holy Spirit. The religious leaders thought He was casting out demons by a demonic spirit called Beelzebub. Jesus responded,

> "Now if I drive out demons by Beelzebub, by whom do your followers drive them out? So then, they will be your judges. But if I drive out demons by the finger of God, then the kingdom of God has come to you." (LUKE 11:19-20)

Secondly, Jesus yielded to God with radical obedience.

> Then He said, "Here I am, **I have come to do Your will**." He sets aside the first to establish the second. (HEBREWS 10:9, EMPHASIS ADDED)

> For just as through the disobedience of the one man the many were made sinners, so also **through the obedience of the one man** the many will be made righteous. (ROMANS 5:19, EMPHASIS ADDED)

> During the days of Jesus' life on earth, He offered up prayers and petitions with loud cries and tears to the one who could save Him from death, and He was heard because of His reverent submission. Although He was a Son, **He learned obedience** from what He suffered and, once made perfect, He became the source of eternal salvation for all who obey Him. (HEBREWS 5:7-9, EMPHASIS ADDED)

On at least three different occasions during His earthly life, Jesus had the opportunity to take a different path than the one chosen for Him as the Son of God. Satan came to Him in the wilderness while He was fasting and tempted Him with power. He offered Jesus the kingdoms of the world if He would only fall down and worship him. Refusing this temptation, Jesus rebuked the devil, and he fled from Him. Satan's temptations were designed to thwart the destiny of God's Son—which was to die for the sins of the world.

On another occasion, Jesus dispersed the crowd that had been following Him because they desired to make Him a king. He realized that if this happened, His destiny on the cross would be hindered. After dispersing the crowd, He sent His disciples across the lake in a boat, and He went to a solitary place to pray. In this selfless act, Jesus showed us the way to respond to temptations.

Once more Jesus faced the temptation to take an alternative route to being Israel's Messiah. While in Caesarea Philippi, He asked His disciples who people thought He was. After some response, Peter spoke out and declared, "You are the Christ, the Son of the living God" (Matt. 16:16). What a revelation! Peter, the rough Galilean fisherman, had figured out who Jesus really was. He concluded that Jesus was the Christ—the Messiah for whom the Jews had waited so long.

Yet, in the next few verses, Jesus began to describe His destiny of suffering and death at the hands of the religious leaders in Jerusalem, adding, however, that He would rise again on the third day. Peter had an understanding of who the Jewish Messiah was going to be, and Jesus' words did not line up with that description. So, Peter rebutted Jesus: "'Never, Lord!' he said. 'This shall never happen to You!'" (v. 22).

Jesus turned to Peter and rebuked him, "Get behind Me, Satan! You are a stumbling block to Me; you do not have in mind the things of God, but the things of men" (v. 23). Why did Jesus do this? He did it because He realized the voice that was influencing Peter—it was the same voice of Satan that had tried to thwart Him since His birth.

Jesus was the ultimate obedient servant of God. When we look at His life, we conclude, "This is what a life totally obedient to God looks like."

> "*The one who sent Me is with Me; He has not left Me alone, for I always do what pleases Him.*" (JOHN 8:29)

> "*If you obey My commands, you will remain in My love, just as I have obeyed My Father's commands and remain in His love.*" (JOHN 15:10)

To Provide an Example of Holiness

The coming to earth of Jesus provided an example of someone living, not only a radically obedient life, but also a life of total and complete righteousness. The righteousness of Jesus actually displayed the very nature of God, into which the Hebrew Scriptures in Jeremiah 23:6 give us beautiful insight:

> *In His days Judah will be saved and Israel will live in safety. This is the name by which He will be called:* **The Lord Our Righteousness**. (EMPHASIS ADDED)

The very nature of God is righteousness. The term *righteous* simply means *right standing*, and, in addition, *right behavior*. If a person is righteous in a godly sense, that person behaves accordingly because that person is in right relationship with God. Thus, Jesus was the ultimate Righteous One. He was tempted in every way that you and I are, but He defeated every temptation.

> *For we do not have a high priest who is unable to sympathize with our weaknesses, but we have one who has been tempted in every way, just as we are—yet was without sin.* (HEBREWS 4:15)

> *Such a high priest meets our need—one who is holy, blameless, pure, set apart from sinners, exalted above the heavens.* (HEBREWS 7:26)

> *He committed no sin, and no deceit was found in His mouth.* (1 PETER 2:22)

Not only did Jesus fulfill the righteous requirements of the law of sacrifice; He is able to sympathize with us *here and now* in the midst of our temptations and trials of life. He isn't like the gods of other religions, which create fantastic deities that take on superhuman characteristics and are far removed from normal humanity. Jesus lived, breathed, walked, and talked; He was tempted and suffered—and overcame it all. He is with us in our daily walk. "Because He Himself suffered when He was tempted, He is able to help those who are being tempted" (Heb. 2:18).

To Make Salvation Possible

The Old Testament law required various types of sacrifices to atone for sin. These sacrifices had to be of a certain type and order. In particular, on one day of the year, the Jewish nation was required to offer a sacrifice of atonement to cover the nation's sin for that entire year. This sacrifice was to be a lamb, spotless and perfect. It is interesting to note that in the Egyptian Passover, as well, a lamb was required as a sacrifice. In the Jewish Passover, God instructed the Israelites to kill a lamb and place the blood over the doorposts of their individual houses. The blood was required to avoid death. Every year thereafter, the Israelites were to celebrate the Passover feast with a sacrificial lamb offered.

That the Passover feast is symbolic of the death of Jesus, and the degree to which it is, is striking. Just as the

Passover lamb was to be spotless and without blemish, so was Jesus. Just as the Passover sacrifice required a lamb's blood to cover sins and avoid death, the blood of Jesus provides an everlasting sacrifice for sins. No other sacrifice is needed. Jesus made the *ultimate* sacrifice. When John the Baptist saw Jesus for the first time on the banks of the Jordan River, he declared that Jesus was the Lamb of God.

> *The next day John saw Jesus coming toward him and said, "Look, the Lamb of God, who takes away the sin of the is the one I meant when I said, 'A man who comes after me has surpassed me because He was before me.'"* (JOHN 1:29-30)

Jesus fulfilled the law of God perfectly. He was the perfect, spotless, and flawless sacrifice. Because of His perfect humanity and His perfect sacrifice, our sins can be removed. "But you know that He appeared so that He might take away our sins. And in Him is no sin" (1 JOHN 3:5).

To Set the Example for the Future Resurrection

The earthly life of Jesus did not end with His death. He rose from the dead.

> *"Don't be alarmed," he [an angel] said. "You are looking for Jesus the Nazarene, who was crucified. He has risen! He is not here. See the place where they laid Him. But go, tell His disciples and Peter, 'He is going ahead of you into Galilee. There you will see Him, just as He told you.'"* (MARK 16:6-7)

The Resurrection proved that Jesus really was the Son of God. If there would have been no Resurrection, there would have been no Christianity. Christianity is based on the reality of this unmatched, unparalleled pivotal event in history. Notice how Paul begins the book of Romans:

> *Paul, a servant of Christ Jesus, called to be an apostle and set apart for the gospel of God— the gospel He promised beforehand through His prophets in the Holy Scriptures regarding His Son, who as to His human nature was a descendant of David, and who through the Spirit of holiness was declared with power to be the Son of God **by His resurrection from the dead**: Jesus Christ our Lord.* (Romans 1:1-4, emphasis added)

The Resurrection was the crowning moment in the life of this sinless, perfect human. The Bible lets us know, however, that Jesus was the first one resurrected, and that many will follow Him in His resurrection in the future.

> *But Christ has indeed been raised from the dead, the **firstfruits** of those who have fallen asleep. For since death came through a man, the resurrection of the dead comes also through a man. For as in Adam all die, **so in Christ all will be made alive**. But each in his own turn: Christ, the firstfruits; then, when He comes, those who belong to Him. Then the end will come, when He hands over the kingdom to God the Father after He has destroyed all dominion, authority and power.* (1 Corinthians 15:20-24, emphasis added)

Jesus is the first of all those who in the future will rise from the dead.

There is one more important note to make concerning the humanity of Jesus. In becoming human, Jesus showed us the goodness of man. Though sin and disobedience wrecked humanity, God created human life and announced that it was good. In fact, the Bible declares in Genesis 1:31 that *everything* God created was good. "God saw all that He had made, and it was very good. And there was evening, and there was morning—the sixth day."

Because people have wrestled with their own imperfections, many have resorted to extreme measures to discipline their bodies. This has gone astray in many instances and has descended into asceticism—practicing extreme forms of discipline to increase religious devotion. Discipline is good; spiritual discipline is *very* good. When discipline is carried out from the perspective that the body is evil, this is not good. Jesus was a real human being and He becomes to us the model of a person created in the image of God. Sure, the world is filled with massive perversions that denigrate the beauty of humanity. However, we should not allow these things to deface the reality of our lives being wonderfully created in God's image.

Jesus is God in the flesh, nothing less. His coming shook the ancient world, and it still shakes the world today. God chose to reveal Himself to a world that was not worthy—a world residing in darkness received the greatest light of all. The Greek theologian, Gregory of Nyssa, beautifully described the reason for Jesus' coming:

> Sick, our nature demanded to be healed; fallen, to be raised up; dead, to rise again. We had lost the possession of the good; it was necessary for it to be given back to us. Closed in the darkness, it was necessary to bring us to the light; captives, we awaited a Savior; prisoners, help; slaves, a liberator. Are these things minor or insignificant? Did they not move God to descend to human nature and visit it, since humanity was in so miserable and unhappy a state?[28]

Endnotes

[18] Quoted in Pat Williams, *How to Be Like Jesus: Lessons in Following in His Footsteps* (Deerfield Beach, FL.: Health Communications, 2003), 281.

[19] John O'Sullivan, *The President, the Pope, and the Prime Minister: Three Who Changed the World* (Washington, D.C.: Regnery, 2005).

[20] [http://amboytimes.blogspot.com/2006/06/mr-gorbechev-tear-down-this-wall.html]. Accessed September 2012.

[21] Margaret Thatcher's speech before the American Bar association in July, 1985.

[22] [http://www.brainyquote.com/quotes/authors/m/margaret_thatcher.html]. Accessed September 2012.

[23] Peter Moore, *A Step Further: The Journey in Discipleship* (Charlestown: Advantage, 2011), 12.

[24] C.S. Lewis, *Mere Christianity* (New York: Macmillan, 1952), 56.

[25] Three of the early heresies concerning Jesus are as follows:

Apollianarianism—The person of Christ had a human body but not a human spirit or mind.

Nestorianism—There were two separate persons in Christ—one human, one divine.

Monophysitism—There was only one nature in Christ. The human and divine natures combined to make a new nature. See Grudem, 555-556.

[26] Ed. John H. Leith, 3rd ed., *Creeds of the Churches* (Louisville: John Know Press, 1982), 30-31.

[27] More detail on salvation is included in the following chapter. Also see Anselm of Canterbury, *The Major Works of Anselm of Canterbury*, eds. Brian Davies and G.R. Evans (London: Oxford Press, 1998), 260-356.

[28] St. Gregory of Nyssa, Orat. Catech. 15: PG 45, 48B.

chapter 3

SALVATION—
God's Greatest Gift

I felt my heart strangely warmed. I felt I did trust in Christ, Christ alone, for salvation; and an assurance was given me that He had taken away my sins, even mine, and saved me from the law of sin and death.

—John Wesley[29]

My favorite holiday of all is Christmas. I love to hear the old Christmas carols, see the decorations in homes and public places, and to gather with family and friends, seeing how everybody looks after another year. However, one of the greatest things about this special time to me is the atmosphere that exudes everywhere. People seem a bit more cordial and polite during the Christmas holiday than any other time in the year. There is an atmosphere of brotherhood.

As a child, my favorite part of the Christmas holiday was opening presents. I could hardly wait to see what was wrapped up in those beautiful packages under our Christmas tree. Even though I am older now, I must admit that I still love opening presents. I still love see-ing those packages under the tree. I now have children of my own, and I love to see them open their presents on Christmas and experience the joy I used to experience when the time came for exchanging presents.

Christmas is just one occasion, one example, that bears out a principle in the human experience that cross-es cultural lines and nationalities—we all love to receive and to give gifts. I believe this part of the human nature comes from the Father of all humanity, God Himself. God is the original gift-giver. As a matter of fact, the true meaning of Christmas is to celebrate the fact *that God is a gift-giver*. At Christmas we celebrate God's greatest gift, the gift of His Son.

Many have said that Christmas is for children. Even though we all know that most adults love receiving gifts on this special day, it does bring a special joy to our hearts when we give children gifts. Why? Children are not able to provide financially for the family. They are dependents. When we give gifts to children, it somehow magnifies our position and ability to provide. In turn, the children re-ceive what they can't provide for themselves and we wit-ness the real power of giving. This small act mirrors God's ability and willingness to give people what they can't pro-vide for themselves.

> *"For God so loved the world that He gave His one and only Son, that whoever believes in Him shall not perish but have eternal life."* (JOHN 3:16)

AN UNDENIABLE PROBLEM

It doesn't take much contemplation to conclude that something is wrong with humanity. Sure, there is a lot right with mankind, but we cannot overlook the wrong—the glaring, overwhelming wrong. If we consider the despotic rule of Adolf Hitler, Idi Amin, or Joseph Stalin, we can rightly conclude that evil does exist and it is often personified.

Modern times have given us a bleak picture of the nature and destiny of man. The eras of the Enlightenment and the Renaissance heightened a creative awareness in thinkers and artists in Europe. Bold new ideas and theories began to emerge. Europe awakened, so to speak, from the period of the Middle Ages with vigor and life. The idea of experimentation took center stage, and the scientific theory became the principal method of discovery. A great sense of optimism prevailed as people discovered they could solve many of humanity's problems by relying on good science, research, and human ingenuity. Social and political theories arose which bolstered the confidence of men to solve their own problems through governmental restructuring.

As time progressed, some thinkers' ideas became more and more pronounced and exclusive. For example, Karl Marx constructed a political theory that he assumed would eliminate inequality and human exploitation. This theory proposed a system that was to be known as communism. Though the concept was intriguing, when it was actually put into practice, it failed miserably. Communism actually fostered some of the evils Marx had originally wanted to eliminate. Again, the problem pointed to an evil within man that manifested in oppression and death.

Consider another radical thinker—Friedrich Nietzsche. Nietzsche called religion on the carpet, as did Marx. To Marx, religion was the "opiate of the masses." Religion was only a tool used by the ruling elite to control the masses. To Nietzsche, religion was part of traditional values that had to be abandoned. He declared the "Death of God." To him religion was mythical, fantasy—something that needed to be eliminated if humanity was to progress. It can be argued that the ideas of Nietzsche found ultimate fulfillment in the actions of Adolf Hitler.

All of the aforementioned show that discarding religion, casting it off as something useless and obsolete, has not solved the problem of evil. In fact, in the wake of the Enlightenment, Europe plunged into the most destructive times ever known to man. World War I and World War II proved that evil was alive and well, even in the midst of great scientific progress. With the Holocaust, the Atom bomb, and the resulting millions of dead, it was obvious to any astute observer that mankind could not solve all of its problems. In the end, science and new political theories had escalated the potential for destruction and provided new methods for men to kill each other. Humankind had emerged out of two world wars with an overwhelming sense of cynicism and loss of faith in progress.

Even today, we witness evil on every side. Genocide is not a thing of the past. One only has to look at Rwanda, Darfur, or the problems in the Congo to see that evil is alive and well. America, the same country that spends more money for the propagation of the Gospel than any other country in the world, is one of the greatest exporters of filth and perversion in the world.

So we are left with questions that have not been answered—as in questions that have to do with evil and its solution. We are in an era of doubt. Who has the answers? Who possesses the truth? The Bible does give us clear answers as to why there is evil in the world. It also gives a clear solution to the problem. Let us be patient. Following is an orderly, systematic explanation of evil and its ultimate solution.

Original Sin

In the beginning, God created the world and all living creatures. This included man and woman, whom God placed in a garden and gave an abundance of good things. In fact, He told them that everything was for their good and that they were to have dominion—or rulership—over everything.

So God created man in His own image, in the image of God He created him; male and female He created them. God blessed them and said to them, "Be fruitful and increase in number; fill the earth and **subdue it. Rule** *over the fish of the sea and the birds of the air and over every living creature that moves on the ground."* (GENESIS 1:27-28, EMPHASIS ADDED)

God also commanded man and woman to not eat of one certain tree in the garden—the tree of the knowledge of good and evil.

The Lord God took the man and put him in the Garden of Eden to work it and take care of it. And the Lord God commanded the man, "You are free to eat from any tree in the garden; but you must not eat from the tree of the knowledge of good and evil, for when you eat of it you will surely die." (GENESIS 2:15-17)

Why did God do this? He did this because He made man and woman people who had the freedom of choice— free moral agents who were able to make moral and ethical decisions. God did not create the first man and woman as robots. He created them to think, to reason, to feel, and to plan. Anything less would not have allowed true freedom.

But God's created beings disobeyed His command by eating of the forbidden tree. As a result, their disobedience tainted their moral character. They suddenly knew they were naked and rushed to find fig leaves with which to cover themselves. This act of disobedience did not just affect them; it affected each person who would be born. Every person that was born after Adam and Eve was born with an inward desire or bent to rebel against God. This is called *sin*.

Technically speaking, sin is "the personal act of turning away from God and His will."[30] More than being an act, however, sin became a condition—the condition or state of all mankind. Since all humans were born of Adam and Eve, all humans inherited Adam and Eve's nature, which was corrupt. The freedom of choice was shipwrecked. Mankind fell. To fully understand this, we will need to explore further the definition of sin and its effects.

For a proper biblical understanding of sin, we must define the term *original* sin. The Westminster Confession of Faith reads,

> They [Adam and Eve] being the root of all mankind, the guilt of this sin was **imputed**, and the same death in sin and corrupted nature conveyed to all their posterity descending from them by ordinary generation. (EMPHASIS ADDED)[31]

The little term "imputed" carries much weight. It means "to ascribe (a crime or fault) to another."[32] As has been stated, mankind's sin nature derived from Adam and Eve. This is called *original sin*. Sin had an originating point from which it was transferred to us—you and me.

Now, let's look at the effects of this *sinful condition* upon mankind. Because of original sin, man is "utterly indisposed, disabled, and made opposite to all good, and wholly inclined to all evil."[33] What a terrible condition.

> *Do not bring your servant into judgment, for no one living is righteous before You.* (PSALM 143:2)

> *When they sin against You—for there is no one who does not sin—and You become angry with them and give them over to the enemy, who takes them captive to his own land, far . . . .* (1 KINGS 8:46)

> *Surely I was sinful at birth, sinful from the time my mother conceived me.* (PSALM 51:5)

The apostle Paul described the condition of *man's sinfulness* in his letter to the Ephesians, "You were dead in your trespasses and sins" (Eph. 2:1), and also, to the Romans, "for as through one man's disobedience the many were made sinners." (Rom. 5:19). The Bible is filled with verses affirming the concept of original sin. We were born in a state of sinfulness, without any ability of our own to change the situation.

Actual Sin

As original sin exists, it manifests in actual sin. How does this happen? For a sin or transgression to be possible, a law must exist which can be broken or transgressed. For example, to receive a speeding ticket, one must be caught exceeding the speed limit law. Thus, the ticket represents a transgression of the law. Sin, in essence, *cannot exist without law.* Just as the speed limit makes us aware of the law's requirement for driving, the law of God makes man aware of His demands.

> *. . . because law brings wrath. And where there is no law there is no transgression.* (ROMANS 4:15)

Paul also states, "I would have not come to know sin except through the law" (Rom. 7:7). So what is the law of God? The law is the "nature and will of God."[34] To break the law of God means to defy the nature and will of God. Now that we understand that sin is a breach of the law of God, we can put forth a definition of sin offered by Charles Hodge in his book, *Systematic Theology*, "want of conformity to the law of God."[35] Hodge said, ". . . the opposite of divine holiness is sin," and if an act or disposition or habit is "opposed to the divine nature it is sin."[36] This really broadens our understanding of this term. Some only think of sin as the big things—such as murder, adultery, and theft but sin involves much more than these.

This expanded idea of our subject is evidenced in a certain New Testament Greek word, *hamartano*, which can be defined as "missing the mark."[37] The term was an ancient term used in archery. The sin (*harmartano*) was the distance by which the arrow missed the bull's-eye. Anything not perfectly hitting the bull's-eye was a sin. So, any act or disposition of ours that does not hit the mark of God's perfect will and holiness is sin.[38]

The Effects of Sin. What are the results, or effects, of sin? What effects does this "want of conformity" exhibit? First of all, *man is guilty before God.* This guilt is seen in the Garden of Eden after Adam and Eve sinned against God: "Then the eyes of both of them were opened, and they realized they were naked; so they sewed fig leaves together and made coverings for themselves" (Gen. 3:7).

Guilt of sin arises out of the "breach of personal relationship."[39] A relationship has been damaged or even severed. Thus, guilt is at the heart of man's transgression of the law of God. "For whoever keeps the whole law and yet stumbles at just one point is guilty of breaking all of it" (Jas. 2:10).

A second effect of sin, in relation to nonconformity to the law of God, is *punishment.* Romans 6:23 says, " . . . the wages of sin is death . . . " Sin has its ultimate end in death. God gave the following decree to Adam because of his sin: "By the sweat of your brow you will eat your food until you return to the ground, since from it you were taken; for dust you are and to dust you will return" (Gen. 3:19).

Death is not the only result of sin. Various aspects of this present life are impacted, as well. This *condition* causes many psychological, emotional, relational, and physical problems. The ultimate, final penalty for sin, however, is everlasting punishment in hell.

> "But I tell you that men will have to give account on the day of judgment for every careless word they have spoken. For by your words you will be acquitted, and by your words you will be condemned." (MATTHEW 12:36-37)

"Then they will go away to eternal punishment, but the righteous to eternal life." (Matthew 25:46)

He will punish those who do not know God and do not obey the gospel of our Lord Jesus. They will be punished with everlasting destruction and shut out from the presence of the Lord and from the majesty of His power. (2 THESSALONIANS 1:8-9)

Three Elements of Sin. How does sin develop? What are its roots? Sin consists of the following three elements: *unbelief, pride, and disobedience.*[40] Paul's words to the Romans are striking: "…whatever is not from faith is sin" (Rom. 14:23). This shows that any action not birthed in faith (or belief in God) is sin. The opposite of belief is *unbelief.* Therefore, any action of man birthed in unbelief is sin. In fact, unbelief becomes the primary source of sin.

Secondly, *pride* plays a significant role in the birthing of sin. Pride was the seat of Satan's downfall. It causes one to center his attention and desires upon himself and his wants. It is a corrupting element in man promoting sin against God. As the words of Jesus declare, "For everyone who exalts himself shall be humbled, and he who humbles himself shall be exalted" (Luke 14:11).

A third element or root of sin is *disobedience.* Disobedience is clearly witnessed in the Garden of Eden when Eve ate of the tree of the knowledge of good and evil and gave of its fruit to Adam to eat. At that moment, both Adam and Eve transgressed God's law and sinned. Disobedience is the actual point of breaking God's law.

What a miserable state of existence. We all have sinned. We all have failed God. In the courtroom of heaven, we all stand guilty and awaiting the punishment that is justly ours—that is, the punishment of eternal torment in hell. This is a very bleak picture. Man is lost without any ability to save himself. Yet, God in His great love and compassion enters the scene with a grand proposition. He decides to bridge the gap of broken fellowship with man. He decides to suffer the righteous punishment of the law in our place. He sends Jesus, God in the flesh, His only begotten Son, to save us.

THE PROVISION OF GOD

God's grand provision for bridging the gap of broken fellowship with man was indeed in the person of His Son, Jesus Christ. A serious, intelligent seeker of truth would likely pose two questions at this point of our discussion: How did Jesus come, and why did He come?

How Did He Come?

In Galatians, the apostle Paul says,

> *But when the fulness of the time was come, God sent forth His Son, made of a woman, made under the law, to redeem them that were under the law, that we might receive the adoption of sons. And because ye are sons, God hath sent forth the Spirit of His Son into your hearts, crying, Abba, Father.* (GALATIANS 4:4-6 KJV)

In this passage we see the "how" and "why" of God sending His Son to earth. First of all, let's consider how Jesus came.

In the Fullness of Time. As some have said, "God is never early and He is never late—He's always on time." In God's great plan to save the world from the terrible condition of sin, He chose the perfect time to send His Son to earth. When a woman is pregnant, the earlier the baby comes, the more the baby will be in danger. Also, the later the baby comes, the greater the possibility of danger to the baby. God, in His infinite wisdom, knew the exact time to send Jesus. He came during the Pax Romana of the Roman Empire under the rule of Caesar Augustus. He came in a time of great Messianic expectation. He came at the *perfect time.*

By God. Jesus was sent *by God*. Jesus was not just an ordinary man. He was not just another teacher. He was not just another healer of ancient times. No, there was something far greater about Jesus—He was God in the flesh. First Timothy says, "And without controversy great is the mystery of godliness: God was manifest in the flesh, justified in the Spirit, seen of angels, preached unto the Gentiles, believed on in the world, received up into glory" (1 Tim. 3:16 KJV).[41]

God did not send His best angel to save us; He did not send a mere human—He came Himself. Jesus was fully God in the flesh.

Of a Woman. This phrase speaks of the humanity of Jesus. Even though Jesus was fully God, He was also fully human. First Timothy 2:5 says, "For there is one God, and one mediator between God and men, the **man** Christ Jesus" (emphasis added).

As a human, Jesus experienced temptations and trials just like we do. Yet, He remained perfect, without sin, during His time on earth. To be a sacrifice for us, He had to be human. To provide an example for us, He had to be human. To rise from the dead, He had to be human.

Under the Law. Jesus was born into a Jewish family, that of Joseph and Mary. He lived as a Jew, kept the Jewish law, and attended Jewish festivals. In Matthew 5:17 (KJV), He says, "Think not that I am come to destroy the law or the prophets: I am not come to destroy, but to fulfill."

Why Did He Come?

To Redeem. Through Jesus, God came to redeem the world to Himself. The term *redeem* actually means "purchasing a slave with a view to his freedom."[42] This redemption was claimed through the death of Jesus. He came to identify with mankind in His humanity and to pay the price necessary to free us from the slavery of sin. "Who gave Himself for us to redeem us from all wickedness and to purify for Himself a people that are His very own, eager to do what is good" (Titus 2:14).

To Adopt. As a part of the plan of redemption, God redeemed us back into His family. "He predestined us to be adopted as His sons through Jesus Christ, in accordance with His pleasure and will" (Eph. 1:5).

God took great pleasure in planning this redemption. Now, we can be made part of the family of God. *Adoption* is a beautiful term describing the intense love of God for humanity.

Jesus was the greatest gift ever given. The Son of God came for you and me. He knew us long before we were born, and He knew we would need a savior. He knew that we would need adoption, that we would need salvation. Now, the question remains: How do we receive all of these benefits and blessings? How do we become part of God's family?

OUR ROLE IN THE PROCESS
(THE PARTICIPATION OF MAN)

Now that we have discussed our condition as sinners before God and the *how* and *why* of Jesus' coming, let us turn our attention to our part in receiving this great gift of God. To enter into the family of God, we must *believe* that Jesus is the Son of God.

> *"For God so loved the world that He gave His one and only Son, that whoever believes in Him shall not perish but have eternal life."* (JOHN 3:16)

In this verse we see the following: (1) God gave to us Jesus—the greatest gift mankind has ever known; (2) This gift came with a condition—we must believe; and (3) If the condition of belief is met, the result will be eternal life and not destruction. Consider how John 3:16 is rendered in the Amplified translation of the Bible: "He [even] gave up His only begotten (unique) Son, so that whoever believes in (trusts in, clings to, relies on) Him shall not perish (come to destruction, be lost) but have eternal (everlasting) life."

Isn't it great when someone gives us a gift that is greater than what we were expecting? God sent us the greatest gift in the world, one better than we deserved—His Son. Yet, we must believe that Jesus was God's Son. To *believe* in Jesus means not only to mentally acknowledge the fact that He is the Son of God but also to *entrust* ourselves to Him.

> *Because if you acknowledge and confess with your lips that Jesus is Lord and in your heart believe (adhere to, trust in, and rely on the truth) that God raised Him from the dead, you will be saved. For with the heart a person believes (adheres to, trusts in, and relies on Christ) and so is justified (declared righteous, acceptable to God), and with the mouth he confesses (declares openly and speaks out freely his faith) and confirms [his] salvation.* (ROMANS 10:9-10, AMPLIFIED)

Secondly, we must *confess* Jesus as our Savior and Lord. To *confess* means "to declare, to say plainly"; it even has the meaning of "to give thanks or praise." When one comes to God, he must *believe* that Jesus is the Son of

God—that He lived, died, and rose from the dead. Next he must confess that fact with his mouth. Believing must be coupled with an open confession of one's belief—to God, at first. In prayer to God, we must confess that we have sinned and that we have broken God's law. It is afterwards that we declare our belief to someone else—that we tell a family member, a friend, a neighbor, a fellow Christian, or our pastor "With the mouth confession is made unto salvation" (Rom. 10:10 KJV).

Thirdly, when it comes to our response to God's gift of His Son, an understanding is needed of what is meant by *repentance*. To *repent* is to "change one's mind, turning about, or turning away."[43] When a person comes to God believing in the Lord Jesus and confessing that belief before others, then he must forsake his sin and walk a different way. It is with God's help that one is able to do this, as it is God who, by His Spirit, initiates the work of repentance in a person's heart.

Finally, we must consider what is meant by *conviction*. In the second chapter of the book of Acts and in the city of Jerusalem, the apostles were filled with the Holy Spirit. Afterwards Peter stood up and began to preach Jesus to the multitudes. The Bible says that the people were "cut to the heart" and asked, "What shall we do?" (v.37). These people felt *conviction* that led them to *repentance*. *Conviction* is "an action of the Spirit that brings about a profound inner sense of guilt before God... [and]... a deep conviction of one's sinfulness and evil."[44] The experiencing of *godly sorrow* would be another way of saying the same thing. Second Corinthians 7:10 says, "Godly sorrow brings repentance."

In response to the question, "What shall we do?" Peter said, "Repent, and be baptized every one of you, in the name of the Jesus Christ for the remission of sins, and ye shall receive the gift of the Holy Ghost" (Acts 2:38 KJV). Conviction had led to the need to repent.

Millard J. Erickson aptly describes this process in pointing out that conversion has two aspects, repentance and faith. "Repentance is the unbeliever's turning away from sin, and faith is his or her turning toward Christ....As we become aware of sin and turn from it, we see the necessity of turning to Christ for the provision of his righteousness. Conversely, believing in Christ makes us aware of our sin and thus leads to repentance."[45]

THE RESULTS OF SALVATION

Again, Millard J. Erickson gives us a helpful assessment of the believer's life after he has accepted Christ and repented of his sins. The beginning of the Christian life consists of the following: union with Christ, justification, and adoption.[46]

Union with Christ

The first aspect of our union with Christ is *judicial*. In God's eyes, when He judges us according to the law, He sees that we are one with Christ, just as righteous as He is. Our union with Christ is *spiritual*, as well, being brought about by the work of the Holy Spirit which is closely associated with Jesus in many passages. (See 1 Cor. 12:13; Rom. 8:9-11; Gal. 3:6; Phil. 1:19.) In a sense, our union with our Lord constitutes our becoming one in spirit. It is not that we lose our identity, but we are somehow in spiritual union with Him. Finally, our union with Christ is vital. The life of God actually flows into our life, bringing renewal to our inner nature and imparting spiritual strength to us. (Rom. 12:2; 2 Cor. 4:16.) Jesus' metaphor of the vine and the branches illustrates this transfer of strength and life. Just as the branch cannot bear fruit if it does not receive life from the vine, so we cannot bear spiritual fruit if Christ's life does not flow into us. (John 15:4.)

> *Therefore, if anyone is in Christ, he is a new creation; the old has gone, the new has come!* (2 CORINTHIANS 5:17)

> *Praise be to the God and Father of our Lord Jesus Christ, who has blessed us in the heavenly realms with every spiritual blessing in Christ. For He chose us in Him before the creation of the world to be Holy and blameless in His sight.* (EPHESIANS 1:3-4)

> *To the praise of His glorious grace, which He has freely given us in the One He loves. In Him we have redemption through His blood, the forgiveness of sins, in accordance with the riches of*

God's grace that He lavished on us with all wisdom and understanding. (EPHESIANS 1:6-8)

For we are God's workmanship, created in Christ Jesus to do good works, which God prepared in advance for us to do. (EPHESIANS 2:10)

For as in Adam all die, so in Christ all will be made alive. (1 CORINTHIANS 15:22)

Jesus replied, "If anyone loves Me, he will obey My teaching. My Father will love him, and We will come to him and make our Home with him." (JOHN 14:23)

Milliard J. Erickson concludes his section on "Union with Christ" by including four implications of this union:

- We are accounted righteous.
- We now live in Christ's strength.
- We will share in His sufferings.
- We have the prospect of reigning with Him.

Justification

As discussed earlier, we were totally guilty before God. According to His law, He cannot acquit a guilty person or He would be unjust. Therefore, because of our union with Christ, Jesus stands in judgment with us and His "spiritual assets, as it were, and the spiritual liabilities and assets of the believer are merged." As a result we are declared innocent in the courts of God because of Christ. God wipes away our sins and the remembrance of them in His eyes.[47]

> *Therefore, since we have been justified through faith, we have peace with God through our Lord Jesus Christ.* (ROMANS 5:1)

> *As far as the east is from the west, so far has He removed our transgressions from us.* (PSALM 103:12)

Adoption

Before we accepted Christ, we were alienated and estranged from God and the life of God. But as a result of Christ's work on the Cross, God brings those who believe into His family. We discussed this concept of adoption earlier as part of the reason for Christ's coming, and need to be well aware of some of the awesome benefits that are included, benefits such as forgiveness, reconciliation, liberty, God's fatherly care, and the Father's goodwill.[48]

Truly, Christmas is the most wonderful time of the year. It is the holiday when we celebrate the greatest gift of all—the Lord Jesus Christ. This is a gift we must believe in, receive, and accept. Then a great transformation takes place in us as a result. We are joined as one with our Lord. He stands in our place at judgment and brings us into the family of God. How thankful we are to our Father for sending us this greatest gift of all—*Jesus*.

Endnotes

[29] John Wesley, Journal entry May 24, 1738, [http://www.ccel.org/ccel/wesley/journal.vi.ii.xvi.html]. Accessed 2012.

[30] J. Rodman Williams, *Renewal Theology*, vol. 1 (Grand Rapids: Zondervan, 1988), 222.

[31] *The Constitution of the United Presbyterian Church in the United States of America: Part 1, Book of Confession* (Philadelphia, PA: The General Assembly of the United Presbyterian Church in the United States of America, 1967), 6.033.

[32] *The American Heritage Dictionary*, second ed. (Boston: Houghton Mifflin, 1985), s.v. "impute."

[33] Leith, 201.

[34] Charles Hodge, *Systematic Theology*, Abridged Edition (Grand Rapids: Baker, 1992), 174.

[35] Ibid., 187.

[36] Ibid., 186.

[37] W.E. Vine, *Vine's Expository Dictionary of New Testament Words*, unabridged ed. (McClean, VA: MacDonald Pub-lishing, 1989), s.v. "sin."

[38] Ibid.

[39] Williams, vol. 2, 254.

[40] Ibid., 230-243.

[41] Also see Heb. 2:14; 1 John 4:2; 2 John 7; Phil. 2:7; Rom. 8:3; John 1:4; Acts 2:30; Luke 1:31.

[42] Vine, s.v. "redeem."

[43] *A Greek-English Lexicon of the New Testament and Other Early Christian Literature*, eds. Walter Bauer, William Arndt and F. Wilbur Gingrich (Chicago: University of Chicago, 1979) s.v. "metanoia." [BAGD].

[44] Williams, vol. 2, 42.

[45] Erickson, 934.

[46] Ibid., 947-965.

[47] On justification by faith, see Hab. 2:4; Rom. 5:1; Gal. 3:6; Phil. 3:9; Heb. 10:38; 11:4.

[48] On adoption, see John 1:12; Rom. 8:15; 2 Cor. 6:18; Gal. 4:5-6.

chapter 4

THE HOLY SPIRIT—
The Empowering Gift

> A religion without the Holy Ghost, though it had all the ordinances and all the doctrines of the New Testament, would certainly not be Christianity.
>
> —William Arthur[49]

No good military commander would send his troops into battle without the proper equipment for war. No good leader would assign his employees to a vital project without the proper resources. In a similar way, God has not left us in this world without help. He has made the power of the Holy Spirit available to us.

It is important to know that when we become a Christian, God puts all of the resources of heaven at our disposal to ensure our success as a child of God. God wants to empower us with His Spirit to ensure that our journey as a believer will be full of joy, peace, and happiness. Therefore, it is extremely important that we know the following: who the Holy Spirit is, that the Holy Spirit has been promised to us, what the baptism in the Holy Spirit is, and how we can receive it. And then we need to know about the fruit and gifts of the Holy Spirit.

GOD'S PRESENCE IN THE HERE AND NOW

Who is the Holy Spirit? Often we think of the Spirit as a mysterious entity that is beyond our comprehension; however, this is far from being the case. To begin with, the Holy Spirit is God—a matter to be discussed further. But, for now, since this is true and God has intentionally revealed Himself in the pages of Holy Scripture, greatly desiring for us to *know* and *understand* Him, we can expect to gain some insight as to the nature of the Holy Spirit. One of the most eye-opening things I ever learned from Scripture was that the Holy Spirit is a person.

The Holy Spirit Is a Person

The term *spirit* denotes "immateriality." A *spirit* is different from a physical being. A physical being has bones and flesh, but a *spirit* cannot be "located, perceived, weighed [or] dissected."[50] Jesus said,

> *"A spirit hath not flesh and bones."* (LUKE 24:39 KJV)

> *"God is Spirit, and those who worship Him must worship worship in spirit and truth."* (JOHN 4:24 NKJV)

The term *spirit* also denotes "freedom of movement."[51] A spirit is not bound to walls and halls. A spirit can go anywhere.

In the world there are many spirits. The Bible speaks of evil spirits that are very real. But God's Spirit, the Holy Spirit, being God, is *holy*—utterly *pure, sacred,* and *majestic!*[52]

But, in addition to the aforementioned in regard to the nature of a spirit and the Holy Spirit in particular, the Holy Spirit is a person. Jesus said,

> *"Howbeit when* **He,** *the Spirit of truth, is come,* **He** *will guide you into all truth: for* **He** *shall not speak of* **Himself;** *but whatsoever* **He** *shall hear, that shall* **He** *speak: and* **He** *will shew you things to come."* (JOHN 16:13, EMPHASIS ADDED)

In this verse, the Holy Spirit is designated by the personal pronoun *He* and the reflexive pronoun *Himself.*

He Is Intelligent.

In other passages of Scripture, the Holy Spirit possesses personal characteristics which point to the personal nature of the Holy Spirit. For example, He possesses intelligence.

> *"For it seemed good to the Holy Spirit, and to us, to lay upon you no greater burden than these necessary things . . ."* (ACTS 15:28 NKJV)

Now He who searches the hearts knows what the mind of the Spirit is, because He makes intercession for the saints according to the will of God. (ROMANS 8:27 NKJV)

He Possesses and Exercises a Will.

Now when they had gone through Phrygia and the region of Galatia, they were forbidden by the Holy Spirit to preach the word in Asia. After they had come to Mysia, they tried to go into Bithynia, but the Spirit did not permit them. (ACTS 16:6-7 NKJV)

And the Lord said, "My Spirit shall not strive with man forever, for he is indeed flesh; yet his days shall be one hundred and twenty years." (GENESIS 6:3 NKJV)

But one and the same Spirit works all these things, distributing to each one individually as He wills. (1 CORINTHIANS 12:11 NKJV)

He Has Feelings.

But they rebelled and grieved His Holy Spirit; so He turned Himself against them as an enemy, and He fought against them. (ISAIAH 63:10 NKJV)

And do not grieve the Holy Spirit of God, by whom you were sealed for the day of redemption. (EPHESIANS 4:30 NKJV)

Likewise the Spirit also helps in our weaknesses. For we do not know what we should pray for as we ought, but the Spirit Himself makes intercession

for us with groanings which cannot be uttered.
(ROMANS 8:26 NKJV)

He Is God

In the previous section, we learned that the Holy Spirit is a person by examining certain of His personal characteristics. Now let us turn our attention to His divinity. Many times in Scripture, the term *Holy Spirit* is interchangeable with God. If the terms *Holy Spirit* and *God* are interchangeable, we must conclude that the Holy Spirit is God. Let us make note of the following passages:

> *Then Peter said, "Ananias, how is it that Satan has so filled your heart that you have lied to the **Holy Spirit** and have kept for yourself some of the money you received for the land? Didn't it belong to you before it was sold? And after it was sold, wasn't the money at your disposal? What made you think of doing such a thing? You have not lied to men but to God."* (ACTS 5:3-4, EMPHASIS ADDED)

> *Don't you know that you yourselves are God's temple and that **God's Spirit** lives in you? If anyone destroys God's temple, God will destroy him; for God's temple is sacred, and you are that temple.* (1 CORINTHIANS 3:16-17, EMPHASIS ADDED)

In Scripture we also see that the Holy Spirit has the divine perfections of God: *omniscience* (all-knowing), *omnipresence* (present everywhere), and *omnipotence* (all-powerful).

He Is Omniscient.

But God has revealed it to us by His Spirit. The Spirit searches all things, even the deep things of God. For who among men knows the thoughts of a man except the man's spirit within him? In the same way no one knows the thoughts of God except the Spirit of God. (1 CORINTHIANS 1:10-11 NKJV)

"But when He, the Spirit of truth, comes, He will guide you into all truth. He will not speak on His own; He will speak only what He hears, and He will tell you what is yet to come." (JOHN 16:13)

He Is Omnipresent.

Where can I go from Your Spirit? Where can I flee from Your presence? If I go up to the heavens, You are there; if I make my bed in the depths, You are there. If I rise on the wings of the dawn, if I settle on the far side of the sea, even there Your hand will guide me, Your right hand will hold me fast. (PSALM 139:7-10)

He Is Omnipotent.

The Spirit of God has made me; the breath of the Almighty gives me life. (JOB 33:4)

All these are the work of one and the same Spirit, and He gives them to each one, just as He determines. (1 CORINTHIANS 12:11)

We know that the Holy Spirit is God because He does the works of God. We also know that the Holy Spirit is

God because He in Scripture is called God, as in *"the Spirit of the Lord," "The Spirit of God," "the Spirit of Christ,"* and *"the Spirit of His Son."* (See Acts 5:3-4; 21:11; 28:25; Matt. 12:28.) We can rejoice in the fact that the Holy Spirit is a spirit, He is a person, and He is God.

The Promise of the Holy Spirit

Before Jesus was crucified, He told His disciples He would be leaving. What a tragic announcement this must have been for them. These men had left everything they had previously known—their jobs, families, and friends— and had followed Jesus for a little more than three years. After all this sacrifice, Jesus told them He was leaving. What would become of them? Would they go back to life as they had known it before they followed Jesus?

Jesus Promised the Spirit Would Come

> *"Let not your heart be troubled; you believe in God, believe also in Me. In My Father's house are many mansions; if it were not so, I would have told you. I go to prepare a place for you. And if I go and prepare a place for you, I will come again and receive you to Myself; that where I am, there you may be also. And where I go you know, and the way you know."* (JOHN 14:1-4 NKJV)

Jesus told the disciples that He would give them another *Helper* or *Comforter*. This *other Comforter* was the Holy Spirit.

"And I will pray the Father, and He will give you another Helper, that He may abide with you forever." (JOHN 14:16 NKJV)

Jesus made this promise before He ascended to heaven.

"Do not leave Jerusalem, but wait for the gift My Father promised, which you have heard Me speak about. For John baptized with water, but in a few days you will be baptized with the Holy Spirit.... But you will receive power when the Holy Spirit comes on you; and you will be My witnesses in Jerusalem, and in all Judea and Samaria, and to the ends of the earth." (ACTS 1:4-5, 8)

This is a beautiful assurance. The Holy Spirit would be given to the disciples to give them power to witness and minister. They would receive power to do what they couldn't do on their own.

The Apostles Received the Promise

On the Day of Pentecost, the apostles received the promise of the Holy Spirit. Suddenly a sound like the blowing of a violent wind came from heaven and filled the whole house where they were sitting. They saw what seemed to be tongues of fire that separated and came to rest on each of them. All of them were filled with the Holy Spirit and began to speak in other tongues as the Spirit enabled them. (ACTS 2:2-4)

Pentecost was a watershed event. The Holy Spirit had come to empower the church and to ensure that the ministry of Jesus would continue. He had come to convict the world of sin and to bring people to saving faith in Jesus. And the outpouring of the Spirit that the apostles experienced on the Day of Pentecost was not just for the apostles; many other believers in centuries to come would receive the Holy Spirit, as well. This experience is called the *baptism in the Holy Spirit.*

THE BAPTISM OF THE HOLY SPIRIT

In the early 1900's a fervor for holiness was brewing among former Methodists in the United States who had broken away from the mainline Methodist church. These people formed several holiness associations and, eventually, denominations. This is known as the holiness movement. This movement reached a climax in a revival that broke out in a little mission church in Los Angeles, California on Azusa Street. The Azusa Street revival was led by an African American holiness preacher named William J. Seymour.

Another holiness preacher from Dunn, North Carolina named G.B. Cashwell wanted to go to Los Angeles to witness the revival at Azusa Street he had read about in a holiness newspaper called *The Way of Faith*. Cashwell was going with the specific purpose of seeking the Baptism in the Holy Spirit.

When Cashwell arrived at the Azusa Street church, he was uneasy at first because of the large number of blacks involved in the meetings. Cashwell was a Southerner and was not used to racially mixed meetings like this. He recalled that a black man laid hands on his head and, he said, he felt "chills go down my spine."[53] Though he was at first prejudiced against the blacks at Azusa Street his interest in receiving the Baptism in the Holy Spirit overcame him. Several black men in the congregation, and William Seymour himself, laid hands on Cashwell. Cashwell said he "lost all pride" and received the experience of the Baptism in the Holy Spirit.

When Cashwell returned to Dunn, North Carolina he rented an old tobacco warehouse and began holding services "which was to result in the conversion of most of the holiness movement in the Southeast to the Pentecostal view."[54] Between the Azusa revival and the Dunn revival, the message of Pentecost and the Baptism in the Holy Spirit spread around the world. What began with a few people at the turn of the twentieth century has now grown into a massive worldwide movement.

As of the year 2000, the Pentecostal-Charismatic movement numbered over 500 million adherents worldwide. That number is projected to grow to over 800 million by 2025.[55] The one experience that has propelled this tremendous spiritual explosion is the Baptism in the Holy Spirit.

This section will deal with the particulars of the Baptism in the Holy Spirit but before discussing this experience, consideration needs to be given to the Holy

Spirit's work in our lives prior to this experience. It is needful that we first lay down the basics of what the Holy Spirit does when a person is converted to the Christian faith.

The Spirit's Work in Conversion

When one is saved, a great work of the Holy Spirit takes place in one's life. As a matter of fact, it is the Holy Spirit who convicts of sin and draws a person to Christ. Therefore, without the Holy Spirit, salvation or conversion is impossible. Notice the following Scriptures:

> *And hope does not disappoint us, because God has poured out His love into our hearts by the Holy Spirit, whom He has given us.* (ROMANS 5:5)

> *Therefore I tell you that no one who is speaking by the **Spirit** of God says, "Jesus be cursed," and no one can say, "Jesus is Lord," except by the **Holy Spirit**.* (1 CORINTHIANS 12:3, EMPHASIS ADDED)

> *And you also were included in Christ when you heard the word of truth, the gospel of your salvation. Having believed, you were marked in Him with a seal, the promised Holy Spirit.* (EPHESIANS 1:13)

> *He saved us, not because of righteous things we had done, but because of His mercy. He saved us through the washing of rebirth and renewal by the **Holy Spirit**.* (TITUS 3:5, EMPHASIS ADDED)

We see in the New Testament, especially in the book if Acts, that the Holy Spirit came upon[56] those who had already accepted Christ as Savior. For example, in Acts 2, the apostles were already believers in Christ. In Acts 8:14-17, the Samaritans had been converted (had become Christians) under the preaching of Philip but had not received the Holy Spirit. In Acts 10:43, the Gentiles in Cornelius' household were already God-fearers (meaning they believed in God), yet they received the Holy Spirit. This actually proved to Peter that they had been saved. Why? Salvation was understood to be a prerequisite to receiving the gift of the Holy Spirit. Also, in Acts 19:2, when Paul visited the Ephesians, he discovered they were believers but had not received the Holy Spirit. This prompted Paul to lay hands on the Ephesians that they might receive this gift.

So, do we receive the Spirit at conversion or after conversion? Yes and yes. The Scriptures plainly teach that one receives the Spirit at conversion. Yet, there has been confusion over this in the discussion of the baptism of the Holy Spirit. The following verses clearly teach that a born-again Christian has the Spirit:

> But you are not in the flesh but in the **Spirit**, if indeed the **Spirit** of God dwells in you. Now if anyone does not have the **Spirit** of **Christ**, he is not His. (ROMANS 8:9, EMPHASIS ADDED)

> Therefore I make known to you that no one speaking by the Spirit of God calls **Jesus** accursed, and no one can say that **Jesus is Lord** except

by the Holy Spirit. (1 Corinthians 12:3, emphasis added)

However, just because a Christian receives the Spirit at conversion does not mean that he has received the baptism of the Spirit. The baptism of the Spirit is an empowering, a fullness of the Spirit, and an open door to the life of ministering in the gifts of the Holy Spirit.

Some in Charismatic and Pentecostal circles understand the Holy Spirit to be given at salvation but not *released* until a later time.[57] Dr. Garnet Pike says the Holy Spirit is already dwelling within the believer because the believer receives the Spirit at conversion. Pike says, ". . . basically all that you are asking for [when you ask to be baptized in the Spirit] is a release of the Holy Spirit to enable you to breakthrough to a new dimension of life in Him. This is called the baptism in the Holy Spirit."[58]

These two views help us to understand two things. Firstly, the Holy Spirit is operating in the conversion of souls. Secondly, there is a *baptism* or *a coming* of the Spirit that every Christian needs. In fact, we are commanded to be filled with the Spirit.

Do not get drunk on wine, which leads to debauchery. Instead, **be filled with the Spirit.** *Speak to one another with psalms, hymns and spiritual songs. Sing and make music in your heart to the Lord, always giving thanks to God the Father for everything, in the name of our Lord Jesus Christ.* (Ephesians 5:18-20, emphasis added)

It is God's will that we be filled with the Holy Spirit. And this gift, just like salvation, must be received—*by faith*. One of the problems many people have in praying for the baptism of the Holy Spirit is the feeling of unworthiness. Such an individual feels that he cannot experience this baptism because he has been such a great sinner or because everything isn't perfect in his life at the present time. The only prerequisite for being baptized in the Holy Spirit is salvation. If we have committed our life to Christ *by faith*, then we are ready to receive the Holy Spirit *by faith*.

Faith requires action. A person receives the baptism in the Holy Spirit by an *act of faith*. When the apostles received the Spirit, the writer of the book of Acts (Luke) realized that the Spirit had come because he saw certain manifestations. The apostles began to speak in other tongues. Something *active* took place. Many people are hindered from receiving the Holy Spirit because they are *afraid* of speaking out. However, we must step out in faith and begin to act on our faith. We must begin to speak *in the language we don't know*. By that act of faith, God will provide the utterance and will fill us with the Holy Spirit.

The Spirit's Work in the Baptism

We have established that the baptism of the Holy Spirit is a work that occurs after conversion or salvation—and a beautiful work it is. Robert W. Graves writes in his book,

Praying in the Spirit, "In my own life, the baptism in the Holy Spirit with tongues has intensified my relationship with the Lord Jesus Christ. Also, it has created within me a desire to minister to the Christian and non-Christian alike. Additionally, I have had a greater awareness of God's will for my life and, as a result, a greater sensitivity to sin in my life. This last effect, however, is wedded, somewhat paradoxically, to a greater realization of God's love for me."[59]

The baptism in the Holy Spirit is promised to every believer.

> *Then Peter said to them, "Repent, and let every one of you be baptized in the name of Jesus Christ for the remission of sins; and you shall receive the gift of the Holy Spirit."* (ACTS 2:38 NKJV)

When we were saved, the Holy Spirit did a tremendous work in our life, but now we must determine to go further in our walk with God. We must pray for the baptism of the Holy Spirit and be "endued with power from on high" (Luke 24:49 KJV).

The experience of the baptism of the Holy Spirit "depicts vividly the idea of being enveloped in the reality of the Holy Spirit. Since to be baptized in water means literally to be immersed in, plunged under, and even drenched or soaked with, then to be baptized in the Holy Spirit can mean no less than that . . . with the Spirit baptism the whole being of a person—body, soul, and spirit—is imbued with the Spirit of God."[60] When we are baptized in the Holy Spirit, God immerses us in His presence and power. Many have testified that this experience was the door through which the other spiritual gifts were released. Once we receive the baptism in the Holy Spirit, we must continue to go deeper with God, and He will release many other spiritual blessings and gifts into our life.

The Evidence of the Baptism of the Spirit

In the book of Acts, when people received the Holy Spirit, manifestations occurred. In Acts 2, the apostles spoke with tongues after the Holy Spirit came upon them. In Acts 8:17, the Samaritans received the Spirit, and even though no manifestations are recorded, they are implied. The apostles evidently knew that the Samaritans had received the Spirit, and Simon the Sorcerer knew, as well.

> Then Peter and John placed their hands on them, and they received the Holy Spirit. When Simon saw that the Spirit was given at the laying on of the apostles' hands, he offered them money and said, "Give me also this ability so that everyone on whom I lay my hands may receive the Holy Spirit." (ACTS 8:17-19)

In Acts 10, Peter and his companions witnessed the Holy Spirit being poured out on the gentile Cornelius' household. They saw the manifestations of tongues and praises to God.

> *While Peter was still speaking these words, the Holy Spirit fell upon all those who heard the word. And those of the circumcision who believed were astonished, as many as came with Peter, because the gift of the Holy Spirit had been poured out on the Gentiles also. For they heard them speak with tongues and magnify God.* (ACTS 10:44-46 NKJV)

In Acts 19, Paul laid his hands upon the Ephesians and they received the Holy Spirit. How did they know they had received the Spirit? "They heard them speak with tongues and magnify God" (v. 6).

Finally, though we have no record in Acts that Paul spoke in tongues, in First Corinthians we see that he did: "I thank my God, I speak with tongues more than ye all." (1 Cor. 14: 18 NKJV).

From these examples found in the book of Acts, we can conclude that when one receives the gift of the Holy Spirit something happens. What was common in the accounts of people being filled with the Spirit in Acts 2, 10, and 19 was that they *spoke in tongues.* Many believers through the years have taken this precedent, that when one receives the Spirit he will speak in tongues, and have acted upon it. Consequently, they have experienced the exact same thing the believers did in the book of Acts. As a matter of fact, this is what began the great Pentecostal revival in 1906. Therefore, when we seek the baptism of the Holy Spirit, we should expect to speak in other tongues.

One of the most convincing Scriptures in support of the Christian seeking the baptism of the Holy Spirit is found in Luke 11:13 KJV, which says, "If ye then, being evil, know how to give good gifts unto your children: how much more shall your heavenly Father give the Holy Spirit to them who ask Him?" The gift of the Spirit is promised to His children. If we are in the family of God, we qualify to be filled with the Spirit.

What is especially worth noting in this verse from Luke is that the heavenly Father gives the Holy Spirit to His children "who ask Him." This is to say that His children do not receive from Him just because they are His children; they must ask, as well. We must make it our goal to ask the Father for the Holy Spirit. [61]

THE FRUIT AND GIFTS OF THE SPIRIT

In this last section on the Holy Spirit, we want to briefly discuss the fruit and gifts of the Spirit. When the Holy Spirit comes into a life, He brings gifts with Him. As He lives in the life of a believer, He will continually cultivate the fruit of the Spirit. Let's look at these two things: fruit and gifts.

The Fruit of the Spirit

A Christian should be known as being different—unlike the way he was before he was converted and unlike the world around him. As we well know, fruit does not grow immediately; its growth takes time.

Let us take a look at and define the fruit of the Holy Spirit, as found listed in Galatians 5:22-23.

> *But the fruit of the Spirit is love, joy, peace, long-suffering, kindness, goodness, faithfulness, gentleness, self-control. Against such there is no law.* (GALATIANS 5:22-23 NKJV)

 Love. Surely love is the one word that above all others should characterize the Christian life. Jesus said that His disciples would be recognized by their love for one another. (John 13:35.) The Holy Spirit develops love in the believer.

 Joy. The Holy Spirit brings cheer to the life of the believer. The believer should be able to stand out in a crowd because he has joy.

 Peace. The Holy Spirit brings healing and well-being to the life of the believer. He brings the peace of God. This is the peace that passes all understanding. In a world full of turmoil and discouragement, the believer is different because the he has the peace of God.

 Longsuffering. Patience is another way of naming this particular fruit. The Holy Spirit brings patience to the believer. To a modern secular world, this concept may seem somewhat strange. Impatience has become a trademark of contemporary society. But the believer is patient.

 Gentleness. This fruit could also be termed as *kindness.* The Holy Spirit makes people kind. The world seems to be ever increasingly hateful and unkind. The believer stands in stark contrast to the world in that he is, quite simply, kind.

 Goodness. This fruit could also be named *generosity.* The Holy Spirit brings a gentle heart to the believer and provokes generosity. In a world of "dog eat dog" and greed, the believer is different in that he is generous.

 Faith. By faith one receives the Spirit and, for that matter, all spiritual things. The Holy Spirit brings and cultivates great faith in the believer. In a world where people do not believe anything until they first see it, the believer believes in what he cannot see.

 Meekness. This term actually means *gentleness.* The Holy Spirit brings the believer a true gentleness and humility. In a world where pride seems to be at an all time high, the believer stands in contrast by his humility.

 Temperance. The word temperance could also be stated as *self-control.* The Holy Spirit brings a sacred control to the life of the believer. The Christian is different from the person in the world who is engrossed in self-indulgent behavior.

The Nine-Fold Gifts of the Spirit

There are many *gifts* of the Holy Spirit mentioned in the Bible. There are three basic lists of such found in the following Scripture references: Romans 12:3-8; Ephesians 4:11-16; and 1 Corinthians 12:8-10. B.E. Underwood describes the Romans 12:3-8 list as body ministry gifts, the Ephesians 4:11-16 list as equipping ministry gifts, and the 1 Corinthians 12:3-8 list as manifestation gifts.[62] Our focus for now will only be on the manifestation gifts of the Spirit that are put forth in 1 Corinthians 12:3-8.

In this aforementioned Scripture selection, there are nine gifts of the Spirit listed. Thus, these are often called the nine-fold manifestations of the Spirit. Let us briefly look at these nine gifts and define them.

> *There are diversities of gifts, but the same Spirit. There are differences of ministries, but the same Lord. And there are diversities of activities, but it is the same God who works all in all. But the manifestation of the Spirit is given to each one for the profit of all: for to one is given the word of wisdom through the Spirit, to another the word of knowledge through the same Spirit, ...* (1 CORINTHIANS 12:4-8 NKJV)

✍ **Word of Wisdom.** "A specific word, given at a specific time, giving God's wisdom to a specific situation"—this is B. E. Underwood's rendering of this particular gift of the Spirit.[63]

✍ **Word of Knowledge.** This gift is in manifestation "when God imparts to a member of the body of Christ information or facts which only God may know in order to assist the church in a special time of need."[64] I've often made note that the Spirit will give one person some previously unknown piece of knowledge about another person to increase that individual's need of faith and to open the way for ministry to him.

𝔇 *Faith.* A special impartation of faith that one receives for the benefit of others—this is the spiritual gift of faith. This kind of faith is different from saving faith.

𝔇 *Gifts of Healing.* Even though healing can come through prayer by any believer, the gift of healing is a special gift for the purpose of bringing healing to others.

𝔇 *Miracles.* The gift of the working of miracles may include various sorts of miracles. According to the Bible, miracles, signs and wonders follow the preaching of the Word. (Mark 16:15-18.)

𝔇 *Prophecy.* "Prophecy is the manifestation of a spontaneously uttered word from the Lord given through any member of the Body for the encouragement, edification, or exhortation of the church."[65]

𝔇 *Discerning of Spirits.* Discerning of spirits is a gift of the Spirit that allows a person to distinguish what is the source of another person's words or actions—whether the source is God or not.

𝔇 *Divers Kinds of Tongues.* Various kinds of tongues is the gift of the Spirit whereby one receives a message to be shared in the context of a church assembly or meeting with other people, with the message meant to be interpreted. The gift of divers kinds of tongues is to be distinguished from the devotional tongues that one receives when he is baptized in the Holy Spirit. As J. Rodman Williams says,

At this point we need to recognize that there is an important difference between tongues as an accompaniment of the coming of the Holy Spirit and tongues as an individual gift of the Spirit... the accounts of speaking in tongues in Acts included all persons present: it was not limited to one or a few... Tongues belong to the ongoing life of prayer and praise. There is no limitation: all believers may speak in tongues...however —and herein is the critical point—by no means do all who speak in tongues devotionally (i.e., in prayer and praise) also speak in tongues for the edification of the body of believers. Tongues in the latter case—"kinds of tongues"—are not spoken by all but only by those through whom the Holy Spirit chooses to act."[66]

Ð Interpretation of Tongues. The gift of interpretation of tongues accompanies the gift of tongues. When a message is given in tongues, then the Holy Spirit will move upon a person, possibly the one who gave the message in tongues, to interpret. Therefore, the whole congregation is encouraged and understands the message—because it is interpreted in English or in whatever language the people speak.

In concluding this particular discussion, it is important to understand that we will operate in whatever gift God needs us to operate for the situation that presents itself. Wallace Heflin, Jr., provides an illustration that offers great insight regarding this concept. Heflin said his dad had a vision years ago of a carpenter's toolbox, and he understood the tools to be the gifts of the Spirit.

He saw there a hammer, a square, a plumb line, a saw, a wood chisel, a screw driver, a plane and several other commonly used tools. When the carpenter goes to his work, God was saying to him, he picks up his toolbox and takes it with him . . . . He may not need everything he carries in the toolbox on today's job. He may only need a hammer and screwdriver today, but he can't be sure. So, he must take the whole toolbox because he doesn't know what job he will be called upon to do today. If he needs only a few tools, he has them on hand. If, however, he needs all the tools in his box, he will have no problem because they are all there available to him whenever he needs them.[67]

Endnotes

[49] William Arthur, quoted in Josiah Hotchkiss Gilbert, *Dictionary of Burning Words of Brilliant Writers* (Whitefish, MT Kessinger Publishing, LLC, 2009), 317.

[50] Williams, vol. 2, 137.

[51] Ibid., 139.

[52] Ibid.

[53] Vinson Synan, *The Holiness-Pentecostal Movement in the United States* (Grand Rapids: Eerdmans, 1971) 123.

[54] Ibid, 124.

[55] David Barrett, *World Christian Encyclopedia: A Comparative Survey of Churches and Religions in the Modern World* (London: Oxford University Press, 2001) 16-18. I am using the term Pentecostal /Charismatic to also represent Third Wave adherents and Catholic Charismatics.

[56] Williams, vol. 2, 190-224. Williams gives the following list of different terms used for the coming of the Spirit in the New Testament: (a) *outpouring*—Acts 2:16-18, 33; 10:45; Titus 3:5, 6; (b) *falling on*—Acts 10:44; 11:15; 8:16; (c) *coming on*—Acts 1:8; implied in John 1:32, 33 and Acts 2:4; 19:6; (d) *baptizing*—Acts 1:5; 11:16; implied in Acts 2 and 10; (e) *filling*—Acts 2:4; 4:8, 31; 6:3, 5:7:5; 9:17; 11:24; 13:52; Luke 4:1; Ephesians 5:18."

[57] Dennis Bennett, *How to Pray for the Release of the Holy Spirit* (South Plainfield: Bridge, 1985). Bennett describes the coming of the Spirit as two parts of one baptism—the first part happening at salvation when the Holy Spirit comes in, and the second part happening after conversion when the Holy Spirit is released and endues the person with power. Bennett explains this by saying "...really there is just one baptism...the inner baptism that takes place when we receive Jesus, when the Holy Spirit brings us alive in Christ and God comes to live in us. This is what makes everything possible...But there are two parts to this one baptism. In the first part, the Holy Spirit comes to live in you. In the second half He begins to move out from within your spirit to flood, overwhelm, drench, soak, overcome the rest of your being, that is, your soul and body, and then move out through

you to the world around you. This part is the baptism with the Holy Spirit" (3-4).

58 Garnet Pike, *Receiving the Promise of the Father: How to be Baptized in the Holy Spirit* (Franklin Springs: Life-springs Resources, 2000), 61.

59 Robert W. Graves, *Praying in the Spirit* (Old Tappen: Chosen, 1987), 59.

60 Williams, vol. 2, 199-200.

61 Kenneth Hagin, *Welcome to God's Family* (Tulsa: Faith Publications, 1997). In the chapter *Why Tongues?* gives the following reasons why every believer should speak in tongues:

1. Tongues—an initial sign (Acts 2:4)
2. Tongues are for spiritual edification (1 Cor. 14:4, 14)
3. Tongues remind us of the Spirit's indwelling presence (John 14:16,17)
4. Praying in tongues is praying in line with God's perfect will (Rom. 8:26-27)
5. Praying in tongues stimulates faith (Jude 20)
6. Speaking in tongues is a means of keeping free from worldly condemnation (1Cor. 14:28)
7. Praying in tongues enables us to pray for the unknown (Rom. 8:26)
8. Praying in tongues gives spiritual refreshing (Isa. 28:11-12)
9. Tongues are for giving thanks (1 Cor. 14:15-17)
10. Speaking in tongues brings the tongue under subjection (Jas. 3:8)

62 B.E. Underwood, *Spiritual Gifts: Ministries and Manifestations* (Franklin Springs: Lifesprings, 1984), 51-54.

63 Ibid., 65.

64 Ibid.

65 Ibid., 69.

66 Williams, vol.2, 397.

67 Wallace Heflin Jr., *The Power of Prophecy* (Hagerstown: McDougal, 1995), 44.

chapter 5

EVANGELISM—
Sharing Good News
with Others

I have but one passion: It is He, it is He alone. The
world is the field and the field is the world; and
henceforth that country shall be my home where
I can be most used in winning souls for Christ.[68]

—Count Nicolaus Ludwig von Zinzendorf

Give me one hundred preachers who fear nothing but sin, and desire nothing but God, and I
care not a straw whether they be clergymen or
laymen; such alone will shake the gates of hell
and set up the kingdom of heaven on earth.[69]

—John Wesley

*R*ichard Wurmbrand was a Romanian pastor of Jewish descent in the 1940's in Romania.
He had given his life to Christ and began to preach under Nazi occupation of Romania. Later the Russians
came to Romania and brought communism with them.
Pastor Wurmbrand began a ministry of witnessing to the
Russian soldiers. He absolutely loved the opportunity of

ministering to the Russians. In the meantime he continued to minister to his fellow Romanians.

The communists eventually took control of the churches in Romania. When this happened Pastor Wurmbrand began ministering secretly to people this became known as the underground church. Because of his activity with the underground church Pastor Wurmbrand was arrested on February 29, 1948 while on his way to church.

Pastor Wurmbrand would eventually spend fourteen years in communist prisons. Three of those years were spent in solitary confinement in a cell twelve feet underground, with no windows, nor light of any kind. During those years in solitary confinement Pastor Wurmbrand kept his sanity by preaching daily sermons that he recalled from memory. He told of many unimaginable tortures that he and the other prisoners endured at the hands of the communist guards.

The most amazing aspect of Pastor Wurmbrand's account is that He and the other Christians who were suffering developed a great love for their captors. They hated communism but loved the communists. Pastor Wurmbrand said, "I have seen Christians in communist prisons with 50 pounds of chains on the feet, tortured with red-hot iron pokers, in whose throats spoonfuls of salt had been forced, being kept afterward without water, starving, whipped, suffering from cold, and praying with fervor for the communists. This is humanly inexplicable! It is the love of Christ, which was shed into our hearts."[70]

Richard Wurmbrand was eventually released because of the intervention of Christians in the West. Afterward he became an advocate for helping the persecuted Christians around the world. His story has encouraged scores of believers around the world who face persecution in their countries. Yet, the outstanding theme that leaps from the pages of his story is the love and joy he retained through his struggles. He had a passion to witness to people and tell them of the love of Jesus in spite of their tortuous treatment of him. This is the heart of evangelism—love for others.

We have discussed the reality of sin and its effects and how salvation breaks sin's power and releases us from its bondage. Therefore, we shouldn't be afraid, intimidated, or ashamed to share the gift of Jesus with His offer of salvation. Telling others about our Lord is called *evangelism*.

THE MANDATE OF EVANGELISM

In Matthew 28:18-20 KJV, before Jesus ascended, He gave a final command to His disciples called *the Great Commission*. Let us look at this passage of Scripture and let it motivate us to action.

> *And Jesus came and spake unto them, saying, All power is given unto Me in heaven and in earth. Go ye therefore, and **teach [make disciples of]** all nations, **baptizing** them in the name of the*

Father, and of the Son, and of the Holy Ghost:
Teaching *them to observe all things whatsoever*
I have commanded you: and, lo, I am with you
always, even unto the end of the world. Amen.
(EMPHASIS ADDED)

Jesus is in total control and is calling people to come to Him. We are just instruments He is pleased to use. Ultimately it is His work. After announcing that all power was His, Jesus told His disciples to "Go!" Because Jesus has all power in heaven and earth, we can go tell the world about Him. He is backing us, and if He is backing us, all power in heaven and in earth is backing us.

In verse 19 of Matthew 28, the term "teach" should actually be translated "make disciples."[71] Our purpose in *going* is to make disciples. A *disciple* is a follower or a pupil. A disciple is one who follows Jesus and, in turn, makes other disciples. Often we make the mistake of thinking evangelism only involves leading a person to a personal commitment to Jesus as Savior. The evangelism call goes much deeper. We are to make disciples of people. Discipleship involves a commitment to Christ, training in how to live as a Christian, modeling the Christian life before other disciples, and teaching these followers of Christ how to disciple others.

The world would be impossible to reach if we, each of us, had to win every single person on earth to Jesus by ourselves. But if we, individually, will win several, who will in turn win several others, who will in turn will win several others, then the kingdom of God would grow exponentially, and it would be very easy to reach the entire world for Jesus. Exponential evangelism will only happen when we catch the vision for making disciples and not just making converts. We need to become *disciple makers.*

There are three major concepts embodied in the Great Commission. I will deal with these out of order for reasons that will become apparent. The first of these major concepts on which we will focus is baptism.

Baptize

> *And He said to them, "Go into all the world and preach the gospel to every creature. He who believes and is baptized will be saved; but he who does not believe will be condemned."* (MARK 16:15-16 NKJV)

Part of the process of making disciples is to *baptize* them. *Baptism* is the "sign both of entrance into Messiah's covenant community and of pledged submission to his lordship."[72] For many centuries water baptism has been *the* primary method of receiving converts into the church. There are two basic ways of looking at water baptism. Firstly, some churches believe that water baptism conveys grace to the recipient and is, in a sense, saving. Secondly, some churches believe that water baptism is *only* a sign of an inward work of God that takes place by way of faith. One should veer from going to an extreme in either of these stances on the subject. On one hand, if we believe that water baptism alone actually saves us, then what role does faith play? On the other hand, if we believe that water baptism is only a sign, then why is it so absolutely necessary? I believe the answer lies somewhere in between these two extremes.

The following statement that promotes a balanced view of our subject is from the Thirty-Nine Articles of the Anglican Church:

> Baptism is not only a sign of profession and mark of difference, whereby Christian men are discerned from others that be not christened, but it is also a sign of Regeneration to New-Birth, whereby, as by an instrument, they that receive Baptism rightly are grafted into the Church; the promises of the forgiveness of sin, and of our adoption to be the sons of God by the Holy Ghost are visibly signed and sealed; Faith is confirmed, and Grace increased by virtue of prayer unto God. . . .[73]

The Smalcald Articles, written by Martin Luther, emphasize the power of God's Word in baptism. An excerpt from these read:

> Baptism is nothing other than God's Word in the water, commanding by His institution. As Paul says, it is a "washing . . . with the word" (Ephesians 5:26). As Augustine says, "When the Word is joined to the element or natural substance, it becomes a Sacrament."[74]

What is water baptism then?

Uniting with Christ.

Karl Barth said,

> Christian baptism is in essence the representation of a man's renewal through his participation by means of the power of the Holy Spirit in the death and resurrection of Jesus Christ, and therewith the representation of man's association with Christ with the covenant of grace which is concluded and realized in Him, and with the fellowship of His Church.[75]

The apostle Paul said,

> *Or do you not know that as many of us as were baptized into Christ Jesus were baptized into His death? Therefore we were buried with Him through baptism into death, that just as Christ was raised from the dead by the glory of the Father, even so we also should walk in newness of life.* (ROMANS 6:3-4 NKJV)

When one is baptized in water, he is united with Christ in His death, burial, and resurrection. In a symbolic way, the baptized person mimics the actions of our Lord's death, burial, and resurrection. The person baptized rises from the watery grave to a new life now being united with Christ.

Faith must be connected to baptism. Water baptism "ordinarily follows upon or virtually coincides with belief."[76]

In the act of water baptism, the candidate has accepted Jesus Christ as his Savior and Lord, has repented of sins, and is ready to live a new life in Christ. The act of baptism is really ineffectual to the person who is spiritually dead, as faith must be alive in the heart of the person to be baptized. However, baptism is not only symbolic. There is a real, spiritual act of God that takes place for the individual involved. The person's faith joins with the act of God in baptism.

A Testimony. In baptism, the candidate announces to the world his commitment to follow Christ. Whether the person is being baptized in a church setting or is being baptized in a river somewhere, the act of baptism itself is a great testimony to the world that this person is now a Christian.

I was raised in the rural Appalachian Mountains of Virginia. Many churches in the mountains do not have baptisteries inside the church. They must use the river to baptize people. I remember on certain Sundays riding down the highway and seeing large crowds gathered on the banks of the river for a baptismal service. Often there were especially moving services involving singing, testimonies, preaching, and so on, and I attended and participated in many of these. These baptismal gatherings at the river bank were public testimonies of faith. The person being baptized was telling the world that he was going to walk with God and live a Christian life. Often people would pull to the side of the road, get out of their cars, and watch the service from an embankment. What a sight! What a witness of one's belief in Jesus as Lord and Savior of his life.

Teaching

A very crucial step in the evangelization process, and the second one that we will discuss, is teaching new believers. Teaching them what? Jesus said to teach them all things that He had taught. Obviously, the teaching content must include the four Gospels. It should include the rest of, Scripture, as well, including Acts, the Epistles, Revelation, and the Old Testament. Teaching the teachings of Jesus is very important because He was God's final step in the salvation of the world. With Jesus there were no more types and shadows. Jesus was the end of it all.

We must understand that the teachings of Jesus are not to be taught to others in theory only—as mere philosophy and nothing else. They are to be taught in applicable ways and are to be obeyed by those who hear them. Jesus' teachings are practical—they work in everyday life.

Go

We will now deal with the first of the three major concepts embodied in the Great Commission. Jesus gave His disciples the divine imperative to "Go." We are to go and take the good news of Jesus and His salvation to all who will hear and obey. The church is to be in motion. The ministers of Jesus are to be in motion. The Gospel must be preached.

> *"And this gospel of the kingdom will be preached in all the world as a witness to all the nations, and then the end will come."* (MATTHEW 24:14 NKJV)

Though it may seem uncomfortable at times to witness to others, it is an imperative. Believers must be living testimonies that speak the Gospel to others.

Now let us consider one other passage where Jesus tells His disciples to whom they should go.

> *"But you shall receive power when the Holy Spirit has come upon you; and you shall be witnesses to Me in Jerusalem, and in all Judea and Samaria, and to the end of the earth."* (ACTS 1:8 NKJV)

Let us break this verse apart and take a closer look at it.

> But you shall *receive power,* when the Holy Spirit has come upon you; and you shall *be witnesses* to Me
> in Jerusalem,
> and in all Judea,
> and Samaria,
> and to the end of the earth.

The first thing Jesus mentions here is that His disciples will "receive power" after the Holy Spirit comes upon them. This is the baptism of the Holy Spirit discussed in Acts, chapter 2. God never gives His people a task without equipping them for the task. God has provided the power of the Holy Spirit for ministry. Though we are weak in our flesh, the Spirit is strong and will do things we could not do.

Then Jesus tells the disciples that they will "be witnesses"[77] unto Him. Here is the testimony factor. The disciples will be living testimonies in word and deed. Next, Jesus tells them where they are to go.

To Jerusalem. The first destination of the disciples was to be the city of Jerusalem. This is where they were when Jesus gave them this command. If we took this command out of its historical context and applied it to our lives today, how would it look? Where do we, each of us, live? We should be a witness first in our local area. This means to our neighbors, to our associates, to our friends and family. If we want to make an impact for the kingdom of God, we must start at home. There are people who need to hear the Gospel who are in our family and our circles of friends. One of the most effective tools of evangelism is new believers winning their family members to Christ. Next, it is new believers winning their friends to Christ.

To Judea. Judea was the larger area or region in which Jerusalem was located. Just as in any larger area or region today, people who live in close proximity to one another usually have similar characteristics, habits, and culture. For instance, people who live in the state of Georgia have a lot in common. Though Georgia represents a wide variety of cultures and traditions, just being from Georgia creates a bond among the people and, for the most part, there should be a prevailing culture. The same could be said of most states in the United States. The easiest people for a person to reach with the Gospel are those who are like he is. If there are no language or cultural barriers to cross, communication is a lot easier. Maybe this is why Jesus wanted His disciples to reach Judea first. The people in Judea were like the disciples. They could speak the same language, they had the same culture, and they were the easiest to reach.

🕸 **To Samaria.** While Samaria was the bordering geographical region north of Judea, the Samaritans were different from the Jews both culturally and ethnically. In fact, the Samaritans and the Jews had a mutual hatred for one another in those days. (See Luke 10:30; 17:12-18; Acts 8:5-8.) Neither did they receive the ministry of Jesus. For obvious reasons, their region represented a more difficult area to reach with the Gospel but an area that had to be reached nonetheless. In Acts we read where the disciples did successfully evangelize these people.

There are places we must reach that may be near us geographically but have people who are different from us culturally. For example, we may live in a city that has a certain neighborhood that is ethnically different from us. This would be considered a Samaritan area.

🕸 **To the Uttermost Part of the Earth.** Dr. C. Peter Wagner has classified four different areas—Jerusalem,

Judea, Samaria, and the uttermost part of the earth— as follows:

> E0—"leading people to a commitment to Jesus Christ who are already church members. As this happens, the church does not grow in membership, but grows in quality."

> E1—[Jerusalem] "means leading people to Christ who are members of the same cultural group. In order to do this you do not have to learn a new language or eat new food or adopt new customs."

> E2—[Judea] "is evangelizing people in a culture similar to your own, like an American evangelizing Germans."[78]

> E3—[Samaria] "Samaria involves a more distant culture such as an American evangelizing Chinese."[79] E2 and E3 "both indicate a cross-cultural evangelism. In order to do it, you have to minister in a culture other than your own.

It is our responsibility to take the Gospel to every people, tribe, and nation. All of us may not be *called* to be missionaries to a foreign land, but if we do not go, we can support others who do go by offering our prayers and finances. We all have the *responsibility* to share Jesus in any setting in which we find ourselves.

⚜ *Circles of Concern.* Each of us has *circles of concern.* For example, if we could write out a Christmas list, how many people would be on it? These would primarily be the people with whom we have direct contact and influence. Each person on our Christmas lists has Christmas lists. If we won all of those on our Christmas lists to Christ, or at least some of them, and if they could win all or part of the people on their Christmas lists to Christ, we would have begun a great cycle of exponential evangelistic growth. A Christmas list is a good example to use for the purposes of our discussion because this would involve for the most part those people who are our close friends and family, the people with whom we have immediate rapport. One statistic says that the average person has about two hundred people in his circle of concern.

Now that we have looked at *why* we should take the Gospel and to whom we should take it, let us consider *how* we should take the Gospel.

THE METHOD OF EVANGELISM

The key to evangelism is being sensitive to the voice of God in talking to people about God. If we notice the way Jesus ministered, He did so in very selective ways. His method often puzzled me. Why would Jesus not line everybody up in Israel and pray for all the sick? Why would He not go around and feed everybody in every village?

The answers to the preceding questions are two-fold. First of all, Jesus said He did what He saw His Father do. The main key to understanding how Jesus ministered to people is that He listened to the voice of God. If God was calling Him to go to someone, He went. This principle is displayed in the story of Jesus coming to the pool of Bethesda in Jerusalem. The Bible states that the place was filled with "a great multitude of impotent folk, of blind, halt, withered, waiting for the moving of the water" (John 5:3 KJV). Jesus did not come to all at the pool that day and heal them. He came to only one man who had been sick for thirty-eight years. Jesus walked up to the man and asked him, "Wilt thou be made whole?" (v. 6). The man made an excuse about having no one to put him into the water, but Jesus responded, "Rise, take up thy bed, and walk" (v. 8).

Secondly, Jesus responded to people often when there was faith present. Many times in the Gospels we see the phrase in one form or another, "Your faith has made you well..." Jesus responded to people's needs with great compassion and at times this caused miracles to occur. In Mark 5:34 KJV, Jesus commended the woman who had been healed of an issue of blood in saying, "Daughter, thy faith hath made thee whole; go in peace, and be whole of thy plague."

In ministering to others, we should be sensitive to whom God is leading us. We should also be open to ministering with more than words. Sometimes God may have us ask someone if we could pray for them. Or we may have a word of knowledge or even a prophecy for someone. Of course, if we don't know this person, we should use even extra caution and wisdom in how we approach them.

A method of evangelism that is re-emerging at this time is to focus on people's physical needs through prayer as a means of opening their heart to the Gospel. Many young people are hitting the streets, going up to people at random, and asking them if they need prayer. Some people are seeing good results from this style of prayer-miracle-centered evangelism. The idea behind it is that the gifts of the Spirit and the power of God are not to be shut up within the four walls of a church but are to be released through Christians on the streets and in the marketplaces of society. The overarching motivation behind this style of evangelism is to display God's love to the hurting individual—to not condemn but rather to show the lost person that God cares about him—and to expect God to touch this person in a tangible way.

Though there are many different tools and approaches to evangelism, the most important thing is not the method but that we actually do it. As we begin talking to people about God, we will learn our individual style, and we will get more comfortable in our own evangelism method.[80]

THE MANIFESTATION OF EVANGELISM

The effects of taking the Gospel to the world will be manifested and experienced in different ways. Three of evangelism's outcomes are that heaven rejoices, lives are changed, and more Great Commission Christians are birthed.

Heaven Rejoices

In Luke 15, Jesus told a story about a man who had lost one sheep, and who left the flock of ninety-nine sheep to go and find the one that was lost. When he found it, he laid it on his shoulders and went home. The man then called his friends and neighbors together and asked them to rejoice with him. Jesus compared this to what happens in heaven when one person who was lost is converted.

> *"I say to you that likewise there will be more joy in heaven over one sinner who repents than over ninety-nine just persons who need no repentance."* (LUKE 15:7 NKJV)

Isn't this a beautiful picture—all of heaven erupts in glorious joy and praise because a sinner repents of their sin? A wayward son is found. A person headed for eternal destruction has turned around and is now headed for eternal bliss. This fact alone should encourage us to witness to the lost.

Lives Are Changed

In 2 Corinthians 5:17 KJV, Paul said, "Therefore if any man be in Christ, he is a new creature: old things are passed away; behold, all things are become new."

When a person repents and accepts Christ, that person is totally transformed (as we discussed in chapter 3). This fact alone, that lives are dramatically transformed, should compel us to be fervent about witnessing for God. We have the news that can transform people's lives. We are witnesses of what Christ can do for sinners. Each of us, if we are born again, has a wonderful gift to give the world. Yet, this good news and gift must be shared and communicated.

I heard a story years ago about an old preacher from the state of West Virginia. The Lord gave him a vision of a dark, cold prison. In this dungeon-like dwelling, the preacher saw many people chained to the sides of the walls with their hands and feet bound in shackles. Then the preacher saw a key appear in his hands, and a voice told him he had the power to unlock the shackles of the prisoners. The old man then began to run as fast as he could, unlocking the chains and cuffs. This story serves to remind us that we have the power to destroy the shackles of sin in people's lives by leading them to Jesus Christ.

More Great Commission Christians Are Birthed

When a person is saved, he should become a follower or disciple of Christ. A *disciple* is one who wins others to Christ. This means that every person we win to the Lord will potentially become a *Great Commission Christian* (that is, a Christian who has the vision to take the Gospel to others). In winning one person to Christ, we have potentially led thousands to the Lord. Who knows when we might lead the next Charles Finney, the next Billy

Graham, or the next Oral Roberts to the Lord? We have unlimited potential to reach the world for Christ's sake.

So let us get ready and GO, realizing that all of heaven and earth is behind us. The Lord Jesus Himself has commissioned us to be His disciple makers, His ambassadors to the nations, and His representatives on earth. We have the news that can liberate the world. We must not hide it. We must not be ashamed of it. We must let it go. As the old song says, *"Get all excited and go tell everybody that Jesus Christ is King!"*

Endnotes

[68] Count Nicolaus Ludwig von Zinzendorf (1700-1760), quoted in Kirby Page, *Living Abundantly* (New York: Farrar & Rinehart, Incorporated, 1944), 322.

[69] From Wesley's letter to Alexander Mather on August 6, 1777. The Wesley Center online at http://wesley.nnu.edu/john-wesley/the-letters-of-john-wesley/wesleys-letters-1777.

[70] Richard Wurmbrand, *Tortured for Christ* (Glendale, CA: Diane Books, 1967) 57.

[71] BAGD, s.v. "matheteuo."

[72] D.A. Carson, *Gospel of Matthew* (Grand Rapids: Zondervan, 1984), 597.

[73] Leith, 275-276.

[74] Martin Luther, *Concordia: The Lutheran Confessions: A Reader's Edition of the Book of Concord*, Smalcald Articles (St. Louis: Concordia, 2005), 279.

[75] Karl Barth, as quoted in Erickson, 1101.

[76] Erickson, 1101.

[77] *Martureo*—"witness"—Meaning a witness to facts, but given by one who is a believer. So the witness becomes an "evangelistic confession." The witnesses have seen the risen Lord and believe in the meaning of it—that Jesus is the Messiah, and now they are to tell others. Gerhard Kittel and Gerhard Friedrich, *Theological Dictionary of the New Testament*, Abridged, ed. Geoffrey W. Bromiley (Grand Rapids: Eerdmans, 1985), s.v. "martus." [Kittel].

[78] C. Peter Wagner, *Strategies for Church Growth* (Ventura: Regal, 1989), 116.

[79] Ibid.

[80] Also see Bill Bright, *Witnessing Without Fear* (Nashville: Thomas Nelson, 1986); Ray Comfort and Kirk Cameron, *Way of the Master* (North Brunswick, NJ: Bridge-Logos, 2006); Bill Hybels and Mary Mittelberg, *Becoming a Contagious Christian* (Grand Rapids: Zondervan, 2008).

chapter 6

PRAYER—
Communicating with God

But verily God hath heard me; He hath attended to the voice of my prayer. (PSALM 66:19 KJV)

What seem our worst prayers may really be, in God's eyes, our best. Those, I mean, which are least supported by devotional feeling. For these may come from a deeper level than feeling. God sometimes seems to speak to us most intimately when He catches us, as it were, off our guard.[81]
—C.S. Lewis

I have been driven many times upon my knees by the overwhelming conviction that I had nowhere else to go. My own wisdom, and that of all about me, seemed insufficient for the day.[82]
—Abraham Lincoln

Every healthy relationship requires good communication. If a married couple stops talking to one another, the relationship is headed for disaster. If a person in church stops communicating with other believers in the church and begins to back away, then that believer is in trouble. Too many times we have seen the believer drift away from other believers, then drift away from church, and all of this is simply a manifestation of what is transpiring in his relationship with God—he is drifting away from God. Needles to say, communication is vital to any healthy relationship.

Just as our human relationships require communication to survive, our relationship with God does, also. Communication with God is called *prayer*. Prayer is a vital key to a healthy relationship with God. The exercise of prayer must be *enjoined on a regular basis*. We should pray *every* day. In prayer, as with communication with people, *quality* is more important than *quantity*. However, the ideal situation is to have both quality and quantity. As a matter of fact, quantity in prayer should breed quality in prayer. The more time we spend with God, the more we will learn how to pray and how to listen to God.

Prayer, however, differs greatly from human-to-human communication. Prayer requires the *faith* of the person praying. Differing from human communication, prayer is communicating with God who is unseen. The person praying must have faith that there is a God, that He can be approached in prayer, that He desires to communicate with us, and that He desires to answer our prayers. It would be quite futile to offer up prayers to a God we did not believe existed or that we did not believe would respond to our prayers. Quite obviously, *faith* is essential in the prayer life of a believer. Now let us turn our attention to the subject of "What Prayer Accomplishes."

WHAT DOES PRAYER ACCOMPLISH?

As we have already established, prayer is a form of communication unlike human-to-human communication. We need to understand that it has capabilities and can accomplish what no other kind of communication can.

Prayer Moves God to Action

Interestingly enough, God has chosen to *hear* our prayers. In the Hebrew language, *hear* not only means to "receive" what was spoken but also to "obey"[83] what was spoken. (See Gen. 21:6; 23:6; Deut. 30:17; 1 Kings 8:30; 2 Kings 19:16; . 2 Chron. 6:21; Ps. 4:1; 39:12; 54:2; 51:8; 84:8; 102:1; 143:1; 145:19; 17:6; Dan. 9:17,19; Zech. 10:6.) God knows all things. He is *omniscient*. Yet, He desires for His people to pray to Him and communicate with Him. We may ask, since He knows all things, why does He want us to pray to Him? The reason is because God has simply chosen to hear His people. He takes pleasure in hearing and responding to His people. Therefore, we should realize that we have the greatest opportunity in the world—we can talk to God. We have an open invitation to approach the King of the Universe, the Everlasting

Father, the All Knowing and All Seeing One in prayer. He is the Creator of the universe and of all humanity, and He has given us the privilege to approach Him in prayer.

Prayer Has No Boundaries

As humans we are limited to whom we can reach for Christ in this life. Yet, God is unlimited in His power to reach people. God can reach anybody, anywhere in the world, at any time. God is everywhere. He is *omnipresent.* For example, if there is a need in somebody's life in China, though we may live in North America, we can pray and God can meet the need of the person in China. Because our God has no limitations, our prayers have no limitations.

John G. Lake was once praying in South Africa for a man who was sick in Minnesota. He entered deep into prayer and felt himself traveling across continents right to the house of this man who was sick. Lake walked up to the man and laid hands upon him, and he was healed. This praying man of God had been translated in the Spirit to Minnesota to pray for a man's healing. Later Lake found out that the man was actually healed at the same moment he was praying. This story shows the limitless boundaries of prayer.

Prayer Accomplishes the Impossible

Since prayer moves God to action and is unlimited in its boundaries due to the very nature of God, prayer accomplishes the impossible. The prophet asked, "Is there anything too hard for God?" (Jer. 32:27). This rhetorical question anticipated a negative answer—*No!* Nothing is too hard for God. No situation is beyond His reach or beyond His capabilities to answer. God is supreme; He is sovereign. He can do the impossible.

There is no sickness beyond God's ability to heal. There is no sinner too lost for God to save. There is no tragedy too terrible for God to intervene. There is nothing too hard for God. Our responsibility is to release all of the situations we encounter to God and allow Him to move. Too often we carry the problem instead of allowing God to carry the problem for us. The words of the old hymn are so true, "*O' what joy we often forfeit. O' what needless pain we bare, all because we do not carry everything to God in prayer.*"

WHAT IS PRAYER?

As was stated earlier, prayer is communication. The most commonly used word for prayer in the New Testament is a Greek word, *proseuxomai*. This term literally means "to pray to God, to pray for something or someone."[84] God delights in us *asking* Him to help us in life. The whole idea of prayer is that of *dependence*. We acknowledge, through prayer, that God is the ultimate ruler of our lives. We are totally dependent upon Him for direction in life, spiritual blessings, material blessings, and just about everything else imaginable. Prayer recognizes that God is in complete control and we are not.

This concept is illustrated beautifully in Jesus' Sermon on the Mount in Matthew, chapter 6, where He taught not only on prayer but on two other aspects of religious duty, as well—giving and fasting. In teaching on each of these subjects, Jesus contrasted how He wanted His disciples to act as opposed to how the Pharisees (the Jewish religious teachers of the day) acted. The Pharisees would give money openly so men could see them. Jesus instructed His disciples to give in secret, or to not let men know what they gave.

Jesus taught similarly when it came to fasting. He shared how the Pharisees would make a public display of their fasting, but how He wanted His disciples to do so secretly. He explained how the Pharisees would pray openly so men could hear them and their long prayers, but He instructed His disciples to pray in private, telling them that God would reward them openly. Then He gave His disciples the example of prayer that many have called the Lord's Prayer.

"Our Father which art in heaven, Hallowed be thy name. Thy kingdom come. Thy will be done in earth, as it is in heaven. Give us this day our daily bread. And forgive us our debts, as we forgive our debtors. And lead us not into temptation, but

deliver us from evil: For thine is the kingdom, and the power, and the glory, for ever. Amen."
—(Matthew 6:9-13 KJV)

Over the centuries, the Lord's Prayer has been one that many have memorized and prayed daily. This is to be highly recommended. I memorized this prayer, have prayed it often, and still pray it with my family. I have found it to have implications and possibilities that go far beyond the few lines that make up its content—something which I dare to say that most, who cherish and pray this prayer, are not aware of. Each of this prayer's six major points serves as categories for communication with God that we can enter into, and each actually serves as a portion of the road map for prayer. Let us make note of how we can organize our prayer time by using the Lord's Prayer.

Our Father Which Art in Heaven, Hallowed Be Thy Name

In the first sentence of the Lord's Prayer, we recognize whom we are approaching and His greatness. God is in heaven and His name is holy. We are not approaching a statue, a rock, a crystal, or some god that only exists in the earthly realm. We are approaching the God of all ages, the Creator, and He is holy.

This phase of this prayer alone can prompt us to pray through the attributes and names of God in Scripture.

Jehovah. "I AM WHO I AM." (Exodus 3:13-15.)

Jehovah-M'Kaddesh. "The God who sanctifies."
(Leviticus 20:7 -8 kjv)

Jehovah-jireh. "The God who provides."
(Genesis 22:9-14.)

Jehovah-shalom. "The God of peace." (Judges 6:16-24.)

Jehovah-rophe. "Jehovah heals." (Exodus 15:22-26.)

Jehovah-nissi. "God our banner." (1 Corinthians 15:57;
Exodus 17:8-15.)

El-Shaddai. "God Almighty." (Genesis 49:22-26.)

Father. (Matthew 6:9; Romans 8:15-17.)

Adonai. "Master" or "Lord." (2 Samuel 7:18-20.)

Elohim. "Strength" or "Power." (Genesis 17:7-8.) [85]

Thy Kingdom Come. Thy Will Be Done in Earth, As It Is in Heaven.

These two sentences, making up the second major point of the Lord's Prayer, serve as a plea that the perfect will of God would be done on earth. This is a prayer for proper alignment—that we would conform to the will of God and that God would intervene in our lives and perform His perfect will. This is the perfect place in this prayer to pray for specific issues in our life and for others that the perfect will of God would be done, to pray that God would intervene and accomplish His will. There are certain issues that we take to God in prayer in which we already know the will of God. For these we simply pray the will of God.

Give Us This Day Our Daily Bread

This third point and plea displays our total dependence on God. What we are really saying is: "Give us today what we need. Provide for us today the things that we need to sustain us and to accomplish Your will on earth." We must stay ever mindful that God is our source and our provider.

And Forgive Us Our Debts, As We Forgive Our Debtors.

This sentence of the Lord's Prayer is a petition for forgiveness. The order is correct—first we ask God to forgive us of our sins, and then we forgive others of wrongs done to us. When we release unforgiveness toward others, we are free to be forgiven by God. Jesus followed up the Lord's Prayer with this statement: "For if you forgive men their trespasses, your heavenly Father will also forgive you. But if you do not forgive men their trespasses, neither will your Father forgive your trespasses" (Matt. 6:14-15 NKJV). We must ask God for forgiveness of all sin and disobedience in our life. Then, as an act of our will, we must forgive others who have wronged us.

And Lead Us Not into Temptation, but Deliver Us From Evil

The fifth major point is a plea for help and protection. Often we ask God to help us fight off temptation and deal with it *while we're going through it*. This is good, but this part of the Lord's Prayer actually asks God *to keep us from it*. "Lead us around temptation, away from it"—this is what we are really asking God to do.

For Thine Is the Kingdom, and the Power, and the Glory, for Ever. Amen

This sixth and final part of our road map for prayer is an acknowledgement of God's authority and sovereignty over all the earth and over our personal lives. His is the kingdom, He has all the power, and He deserves all the glory. We can conclude our time of prayer with worship—just spending time praising God for answering our prayers and for being Lord over every situation in our lives.

HOW DO WE PRAY?

The great Protestant Reformer, John Calvin, also gives us helpful tips on how to pray. The following are modifications of Calvin's teachings on prayer with Calvin's words remaining in parentheses.

Focus Your Mind on God (Have our heart and mind framed as becomes those who are entering into converse with God.) [86]

In prayer we must focus our thoughts on God. This is a real challenge to prayer. Many times the phone distracts us, or the children, or something else. We must try to find a quiet place where we will be uninterrupted to pray.

Pray According to God's Will (We are to ask only in so far as God permits.) [87]

God wants us to pray to Him openly and honestly, but He also wants us to pray in agreement with His will. This comes through study of the Bible and by allowing the Holy Spirit to pray through us. Notice how the following Scripture references admonish this very thing:

> *Now this is the confidence that we have in Him, that if we ask anything according to His will, He hears us.* (1 JOHN 5:14 NKJV)

> *Likewise the Spirit also helps in our weaknesses. For we do not know what we should pray for as we ought, but the Spirit Himself makes intercession for us with groanings which cannot be uttered.* (ROMANS 8:26 NKJV)

Pray Earnestly, Sincerely in Faith Believing (In asking we must truly feel our wants, and seriously considering that we need all the things which we ask, accompany the prayer with a sincere, nay, ardent desire of obtaining them.) [88]

Calvin is expressing, in a very eloquent way, that our prayers are not to be cold, detached, and just mumblings we have memorized. Our prayers are to be sincere; we must feel the need for the things we ask. Notice what James 5:16 NKJV says: "Confess your trespasses to one another, and pray for one another, that you may be healed. The effective, fervent prayer of a righteous man avails much."

Don't Pray Selfish Prayers (He who comes into the presence of God to pray must divest himself of all vainglorious thoughts.) [89]

Calvin goes on to say, "Discard all self-confidence, humbly giving God the whole glory, lest by arrogating anything, however little, to himself, vain pride cause him to turn away his face."[90] God opposes pride. An important reason why we serve God is because we have come to the realization that we are not self-sufficient beings. We have realized that we cannot save ourselves. We have been awakened to the fact that God alone can save, and we humbly cast all of our cares upon Him and trust Him for help. This is the essence of prayer. How ridiculous would it be to come before God in a prideful and arrogant posture.

Again, Have Faith (We should be animated to pray with the sure hope of succeeding.) [91]

In short, when it comes to prayer, the extreme importance of faith cannot be overlooked or minimized. We should believe that our prayers are being heard and that God is able and willing to answer them. In Mark 11:24 NKJV, we read: "Therefore I say to you, whatever things you ask when you pray, believe that you receive *them*, and you will have *them*."

Finally, there is one more thought from Calvin which is helpful. Many give up on prayer because they fail in some way in the Christian life. Often people stumble, commit old sins, struggle with evil thoughts, and wrestle with feelings of anger, depression, or despair. As a result individuals often feel unworthy to pray, or they feel that God will not hear them because of their wickedness. Calvin says,

> Genuine prayer is not that by which, while confessing our guilt, we utter our sorrows before God, just as children familiarly lay their complaints before their parents. Nay, the immense accumulation of our sins should rather spur us on and incite us to prayer... I confess, indeed that these stings would prove mortal darts, did not God give succour [help]; but our heavenly Father has, ineffable kindness, added a remedy, by which, calming all perturbation [agitation], soothing our cares, and dispelling our fears, he condescendingly allures us to himself; nay, removing all doubts, not to say obstacles, makes the way smooth before us." [92]

Though we are not perfect, God still makes the path smooth before us (Ps. 27:11) to come into His presence and pray. What a privilege, what an honor, to pray openly and honestly to a Father who cares and responds.

FASTING—WHY DO IT?

No discussion of biblical prayer would be complete without mentioning fasting. When Jesus taught the Sermon on the Mount, He outlined three basic disciplines that are expected to be in the life of a Christian— prayer, fasting, and giving. He criticized the hypocrisy of those who do these disciplines for show or to gain applause from men. Jesus' teaching focused on the proper motive behind these three disciplines—humility. This is illustrated below:

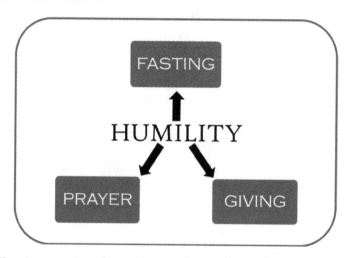

Fasting is simply going without food to focus upon a spiritual purpose. When we forgo eating, our mind is able to focus on God. Granted, we need to be wise in attempting to fast. If we have medical problems, we should be extra careful. Fasting is not a punishment; it is to be a help. It takes our focus away from food and our own physical needs and allows us to focus on our spiritual needs. There is even a lot of good research that confirms the benefits of fasting for the physical body.

In the Bible, several different fasts are mentioned. The most basic of these is simply doing without food for a period of time. This is called a pure fast—eating nothing and drinking nothing except water. Some individuals in the Bible fasted for forty days—such as Moses and Jesus. Fasting was also a weekly discipline of the Jewish Pharisees. It was a sign of mourning, also. The nation of Israel fasted corporately at times. There were also limited fasts, such as Daniel's fast where he only ate certain types of food (Dan. 10:2-3).

There are different kinds of fasts and there are different reasons for fasting. We need to understand more particularly some of these reasons.

Jesus Did It

Of course, Jesus is the ultimate example of how one should live. It is noted in Matthew 4:1-2 NKJV that fasting was part of His life: "Then Jesus was led up by the Spirit into the wilderness to be tempted by the devil. And when He had fasted forty days and forty nights, afterward He was hungry."

We Are Told To Do It

As has been mentioned earlier, prayer, giving, and fasting are three disciplines that Jesus speaks of in Matthew, chapter 6. In His teaching, He assumes that these are the regular disciplines of a believer.

> *"Moreover, when you fast, do not be like the hypocrites, with a sad countenance. For they disfigure their faces that they may appear to men to be fasting. Assuredly, I say to you, they have their reward. But you, when you fast, anoint your head and wash your face, so that you do not appear to men to be fasting, but to your Father who is in the secret place; and your Father who sees in secret will reward you openly."* (MATTHEW 6:16-18 NKJV)

People in the Bible Did It

Many of the individuals in the Bible provide a wonderful example of fasting for us. Following are a few: Moses (Ex. 34:28), Elijah (1 Kgs. 19:8), Ezra (Ezra 10:6), Daniel (Dan. 10:3), Paul (Acts 9:9), leaders in the church at Antioch (Acts 13:2), and Paul and Barnabus (Acts 14:23).

Fasting Brings Miracles (Isaiah 58)

Many great men and women of God throughout history fasted as part of their spiritual life, and, as a result, they discovered great power with God. In Isaiah 58, mention is made of fasting and some amazing spiritual benefits this discipline can bring. Of course, the context of this passage is that fasting should be coupled with a devoted and generous life. Here are some of the benefits mentioned:

- ❦ *Healing*
- ❦ *Restoration of Righteousness*
- ❦ *Welcomes the Glory of the Lord*
- ❦ *Brings Answers to Prayer*
- ❦ *Removes Gloom*
- ❦ *Brings Guidance*
- ❦ *Satisfies Your Soul*
- ❦ *Brings Strength to Bones*
- ❦ *Makes You a Watered Garden*
- ❦ *Rebuilds Ancient Ruins*
- ❦ *Lays a Foundation for Future Generations*
- ❦ *Repairs the Breach.*

Fasting Brings the Victory (2 Chronicles 20)

This brings us to a final and interesting concept about fasting. In 2 Chronicles 20, the kingdom of Judah found itself surrounded by invading armies, which were much larger and more powerful than that of Judah. The king, Jehoshaphat, made a brilliant move—he called a prayer meeting and a time of fasting. "And Jehoshaphat feared, and set himself to seek the Lord, and proclaimed a fast throughout all Judah." (v. 3, KJV)As a result of this time of fasting and prayer, God spoke to the king through a prophet named Jehaziel, giving the king comfort and instructions on how to fight the enemy. Jehoshaphat sent his armies into battle with people on the front line praising God in worship. God "set ambushments" (v. 22) against the enemy, and when Judah entered the battle zone, all of its enemies had fled. All that remained to be done was to gather the spoil.

Fasting brings victory into our lives. If we have been bound (literally attacked) by things that are stronger than us, we should try fasting as an offensive weapon. We should submit ourselves unto God and then let Him fight the battles for us. God told Jehoshaphat that day, "You will not *need* to fight in this *battle*. Position yourselves, stand still and see the salvation of the Lord, who is with you, O Judah and Jerusalem!' Do not fear or be dismayed; tomorrow go out against them, for the Lord *is* with you" (v. 17).

HOW TO HEAR GOD'S VOICE

Just as fasting is a vital aspect of biblical prayer, no presentation of this subject would be complete without discussing how we can hear God's voice. One of the greatest things a Christian can learn to do is to hear God's voice. Jesus said, "And when he [the true Shepherd] brings out his own sheep, he goes before them; and the sheep follow him, *for they know his voice.* Yet they will by no means follow a stranger, but will flee from him, for they do not know the voice of strangers" (John 10:4-5 NKJV, emphasis added). This gives us the comfort of knowing that Jesus is speaking to us. Some believe that God no longer speaks to people but made the Scriptures His final word to man. Yet this isn't so. God spoke to men and women of God all throughout the Bible, and He still does so today. Let us be sensitive to the voice of God in our life and learn to hear from Him. With all of the competing voices in our head, our task is to simply discern which voice is His. Following are a few simple guidelines that can help us discern whether God is speaking to us or not:

1. Does the thought you are having sound like something Jesus would say?
2. Does the thought you are having agree with the whole Word of God (the Bible)?
3. Does the voice you are hearing bring you comfort and reassurance or is it disturbing?
4. Does the voice you are hearing bind you through legalism or set you free?

Prayer—it is our lifeline to God. One of the greatest privileges we have in being a Christian is that of prayer. Martin Luther said, "Prayer is not overcoming God's reluctance, but laying hold of His willingness."

To conclude our discussion of prayer it would be good to look at an example of a praying person. George Müller was a Christian pastor who lived in the nineteenth century (1805-1898). Though born in Prussia, he ended up in Bristol, England pastoring and operating an orphanage. Müller had a very simple faith and trust in God. He set four rules for his life and ministry: (1) Not to receive any fixed salary; (2) Never to ask any human being for help;

(3) To, literally, *"Sell what you have and give alms;"* and (4) To, literally, *"Owe no man anything"* (Rom. 13:8).

Müller was compelled to start an orphanage after walking the streets seeing children everywhere who had no parents. These children lived on the streets or in government run poor houses. Müller prayed for God to provide a building for the orphanage and for the people to oversee its operation. God provided.

Müller ran his orphanage completely by faith. For ten years, the supplies for the orphanage were received from God through prayer. Money came from different sources. Sometimes, down to nothing, Müller would pray and the supplies the children needed would come at the last moment. He lived completely by faith and prayer.

Müller kept a notebook where he would record his petitions to the Lord on one page. One the other page he would record the answer to the prayer. By doing this he was able to document specific answers to his prayers. Müller affirmed that he had received over 50,000 specific answers to prayer. Many of these, 5,000 or so, had been answered on the day he prayed. He said, "When once I am persuaded that a thing is right and for the glory of God, I go on praying for it until the answer comes. George Müller never gives up!" [93]

Müller saw over 10,000 children come through his orphanage. "When each child became old enough to live on his own, George would pray with him and put a Bible in his right hand and a coin in his left. He explained to the young person that if he held onto what was in his right hand, God would always make sure there was something in his left hand as well."[94] This great work was accomplished through the power of a dedicated, praying man.

Endnotes

[81] C.S. Lewis, *Letters to Malcolm: Chiefly on Prayer* (New York: Harcourt, Inc. 2002), 116-117.

[82] *Lincoln Observed: The Civil War Dispatches of Noah Brooks*, ed. Michael Burlingame (Baltimore, Johns Hopkins University Press, 1998), 210.

[83] *The New Brown-Driver-Briggs-Gesenius Hebrew and English Lexicon* (Peabody, MA.: Hendrickson, 1979), s.v. "shema," #8085. [BDB].

[84] BAGD, s.v. "prosuexomai."

[85] Basic definitions and scriptural references are taken from The Navigators, "Thirty Days of Praying the Names and Attributes of God," 2012, [http://www.navigators.org/us/resources/ items/Thirty%20Days%20of%20Praying%20the%20Names%20and%20Attributes%20of%20God], Accessed September 2012.

[86] John Calvin, *Institutes of the Christian Religion*, Book 3, trans. Henry Beveridge (Grand Rapids: Zondervan, 1995), 20:12. All of the above points of prayer are taken from the same chapter.

[87] Ibid.

[88] Ibid.

[89] Ibid.

[90] Ibid.

[91] Ibid.

[92] John Calvin, 20:12. All of the above points of prayer are taken from the same chapter.

[93] [http://www.keepandshare.com/doc4/1488/one-of-the-most-moving-stories-of-faith-i-have-ever-read?p=y]. Accessed 2013. Also see George Müller, *Answers to Prayer* (Feather Trail Press, 2010).

[94] George Mueller, *Orphanages Built by Prayer.* [http://www.christianity.com/church/church-history/church-history-for-kids/george-mueller-orphanages-built-by-prayer-11634869.html] Accessed 2013.

chapter 7

HEALING—
A Christian's Blessing

"But I will restore you to health and heal your wounds," declares the Lord. (JEREMIAH 30:17)

If it is not God's will for you to be well, it would be wrong for you to seek recovery even through natural means.[95]

—T. L Osborne

How many times have people questioned the idea of healing? This subject has been the catalyst for many discussions and debates. The human race has wrestled with horrendous disease and suffering for most of its existence. Why some individuals are healed while others are not is a difficult question in the mind of most. Regardless, Scripture clearly reveals God as a healer and has much to say about healing, as it provides many answers to the human dilemma of suffering due to sickness. Let us now focus on this wonderful subject of divine healing.

GOD IS A HEALER

One of the greatest revelations in Scripture is that God is a healer. His very nature is that of a healer. In the book of Exodus, we see Him revealed this way:

> He said, 'If you listen carefully to the voice of the Lord your God and do what is right in His eyes, if you pay attention to His commands and keep all His decrees, I will not bring on you any of the diseases I brought on the Egyptians, for **I am the Lord, who heals you.**'" (Exodus 15:26, emphasis added)

Here the expression used for God is Jehovah-Rapha, meaning, *"The God that heals you."* What is interesting about this is that healing isn't just an act that God performs; it is actually His nature. God is a healer. God created the world, and since He is a healer, He created healing as a process in nature. There are many things that have healing properties and many different healing processes are found in living beings.

Disease and sickness entered into the earth realm because of sin. I do not believe Adam and Eve would have ever dealt with sickness had they not sinned. God's judgment upon them was death. Granted, they did not die immediately, but they did die eventually. Death entered the earth realm as access to the Tree of Life was severed.

Healing was a major part of the life and ministry of Jesus. If we study the four Gospels, we find that a large amount of the text is given to healing miracles. Jesus healed lepers, the blind, the lame, withered hands, sicknesses that were fatal, and so on.

> *Jesus went throughout Galilee, teaching in their synagogues, preaching the good news of the kingdom, and healing every disease and sickness among the people. News about Him spread all over Syria, and people brought to Him all who were ill with various diseases, those suffering severe pain, the demon-possessed, those having seizures, and the paralyzed, and He healed them.* (MATTHEW 4:23-24)

There was no disease that Jesus couldn't heal. In fact, the only instance given in the Gospels where Jesus did not do a lot of miracles was when He visited His hometown of Nazareth, and we are given a reason for this—the people did not have faith.

> *Jesus said to them, "Only in his hometown, among his relatives and in his own house is a prophet without honor." He could not do any miracles there, except lay His hands on a few sick people and heal them. And He was amazed at their lack of faith.* (MARK 6:4-6)

FAITH IS CONNECTED TO HEALING

It is obvious in Scripture that there is a connection between faith and healing. In many cases, Jesus and the apostles related a healing miracle to the person's faith to be healed. In Acts 3:16, we see this illustrated: "By faith in the name of Jesus, this man whom you see and know was made strong. It is Jesus' name and the faith that comes through Him that has given this complete healing to him, as you can all see."

Jesus said to the woman with the bleeding disorder who had pressed through the crowd just to touch the fringe of His garment, "'Take heart, daughter,' He said, 'your faith has healed you.' And the woman was healed from that moment" (Matt. 9:22). When the Canaanite woman came to Jesus and begged Him to heal her daughter, He said, "'Woman, you have great faith. Your request is granted.' And her daughter was healed from that very hour" (Matt. 15:28). When the blind beggar desperately sought his healing from Jesus, "Jesus said to him, 'Receive your sight; your faith has healed you.' Immediately he received his sight and followed Jesus, praising God. When all the people saw it, they also praised God" (Luke 18:42-43).

In the previous passages, faith plays a significant role in healing. In fact, in several of the healing miracles in the Bible, faith was the *cause* of the miracle. Faith was the catalyst. This is not obvious in every case, but it is plain in many cases. *God honors faith.*

We may be wondering how we can get faith? The Bible states, "So then faith *comes* by hearing, and hearing by the word of God" (Rom. 10:17 NKJV). To encourage our faith, the following is some of the things we can do: listen to good biblical preaching, read the Scriptures on a regular basis, study the Scriptures in an in-depth manner, and listen to Gospel music that communicates the positive message of the Bible. When we read or hear of the things God has done in the past, it will encourage us to believe for things God can do in the future.

BIBLICAL REASONS TO PRACTICE HEALING

The biblical reasons are many as to why someone, the Christian, in particular, should believe for healing and even expect to be used of God as an instrument of administering healing to others. Following is a discussion of some of those reasons.

The Nation of Israel Experienced God's Healing

In Exodus 23:25, God told the nation of Israel, "Worship the Lord your God, and His blessing will be on your food and water. I will take away sickness from among you." Israel was given a magnificent promise regarding healing. In Exodus 15, God had revealed His nature as a healer to these people. He also gave them a promise that He would take sickness and disease away from them. It is true that the Israelites experienced the healing power of God in many instances, as when they wandered through the wilderness for forty years, and were protected from sickness and disease.

If Israel was truly the people of God in covenant with God, then the church is the people of God in covenant with God according to the New Testament. Thus, why can't we have faith in the same God of healing that the Israelites had? God has not changed. In fact, since God is eternal, if He revealed Himself as a healer to the Israelites, *He will always be a healer to every generation.* This is why healing was such a major part of Jesus' ministry—it was the nature of God being displayed and manifested.

The Apostles Ministered to the Sick

The apostles followed in the footsteps of Jesus. They healed the sick just as Jesus had healed sick. The book of Acts is filled with healing miracles performed at the hands of the apostles. In fact, in one of Peter's sermons, he referred to Jesus, explaining, "How God anointed Jesus of Nazareth with the Holy Spirit and power, and how He went around doing good and healing all who were under the power of the devil, because God was with Him" (Acts 10:38). Two interesting facts jump out at us from this verse—firstly, good is equivalent to healing the oppressed; secondly, oppression is linked to the work of the devil. This is simple theology here—God is good; the devil is bad. Logically, we could take this a step further—God does good; the devil does bad.

Peter and John continued the healing ministry of Jesus by healing the lame man at the temple gate, as recorded in Acts 3. They were later chastised for this miracle and, as a result, went back and held a prayer meeting in which they asked God, "Stretch out Your hand to heal and perform miraculous signs and wonders through the name of Your holy servant Jesus" (Acts 4:30). They were so bold and so excited they wanted to go do more. The reputation of the apostles grew, and people knew that miracles flowed through their hands. "The apostles performed many miraculous signs and wonders among the people. And all the believers used to meet together in Solomon's Colonnade. No one else dared join them, even though they were highly regarded by the people" (Acts 5:12-13).

Yet, miracles were not relegated to the Apostles only. Other believers performed miracles in the book of Acts. Philip was appointed as a deacon and went to Samaria and preached Jesus. The result was a massive revival accompanied by miracles. "When the crowds heard Philip and saw the miraculous signs he did, they all paid close attention to what he said. With shrieks, evil spirits came out of many, and many paralytics and cripples were healed. So there was great joy in that city" (Acts 8:6-8).

Paul was another apostle, though not one of the original twelve, who healed the sick.

There was an estate nearby that belonged to Publius, the chief official of the island. He welcomed us to his home and for three days entertained us hospitably. His father was sick in bed, suffering from fever and dysentery. Paul went in to see him and, after prayer, placed his hands on him and healed him. When this had happened, the rest of the sick on the island came and were cured. (ACTS 28:7-9)

In Lystra there sat a man crippled in his feet, who was lame from birth and had never walked. He listened to Paul as he was speaking. Paul looked directly at him, saw that he had faith to be healed and called out, "Stand up on your feet!" At that, the man jumped up and began to walk. (ACTS 14:8-10)

Notice the bold command of Paul, "Stand up on your feet!" In studying great healing ministers and revivals in the past, I have noticed that often the person in need of healing was required to do something physically to show his faith was active. Jesus commanded, *Take up your bed and walk*, or *Stretch forth your hand*, or even *Roll the stone away*. If one really believes in something, he will act on it. For example, if we are into investing and we think a company is set to successfully take off within the next year, we would invest in that company. We would take action based upon our belief. Healing works in a similar way. If we believe God for our healing, we should pray and then take action based upon our faith.

We Are Commanded in the Church to Pray for the Sick

Any believer in Jesus can pray for healing. First of all, we can pray for healing based upon faith in God's Word. Secondly, the sick can call upon church leadership to prayer for them, as James 5:14 tells us: "Is any one of you sick? He should call the elders of the church to pray over him and anoint him with oil in the name of the Lord." Thirdly, believers can lay hands on the sick.

> *"And these signs will accompany* **those who believe:** *In My name they will drive out demons; they will speak in new tongues; they will pick up snakes with their hands; and when they drink deadly poison, it will not hurt them at all; they will place their hands on sick people, and they will get well."* (MARK 16:17-18, EMPHASIS ADDED)

Fourthly, some believers may operate in the *gifts of healing.*

> *To one there is given through the Spirit the message of wisdom, to another the message of knowledge by means of the same Spirit, to another faith by the same Spirit,* **to another gifts of healing by that one Spirit,** *to another miraculous powers, to another prophecy, to another distinguishing between spirits, to another speaking in different kinds of tongues, and to still another the interpretation of tongues.* (1 CORINTHIANS 12:8-10, EMPHASIS ADDED)

Healing Is a Part of the Gospel of Christ

Healing *is* the Gospel message. Jesus came to heal the world of a broken relationship with God. Jesus also came to heal the sick. When He sent out seventy to minister in His name, He instructed them to do the following: "When you enter a town and are welcomed, eat what is set before you. Heal the sick who are there and tell them, 'The kingdom of God is near you'" (Luke 10:8-9).

Notice that healing was coupled with telling the people that the kingdom of God is near. Healing was paired with preaching. Jesus went forth both *doing* and *teaching* (Acts 1:1). Healing is as much a part of the Gospel as preaching.

IS HEALING FOR ALL?

There has been quite a bit of debate concerning the question, "Is healing for all?" This has turned into a tension-filled problem in some circles. Why? Many people have prayed for healing and have not received, and others, in turn, have accused these of not having faith for their healing. Those who were not healed have often been crushed by such accusations. The sick have often prayed with great and sincere desire to be healed but have walked away still sick. As has already been established, healing is part of the Gospel. Thus, we can firmly say that healing *is* God's will. Yet, in reality, some are not healed. What is the answer to this dilemma?

Sometimes People Are Not Healed Because They Have Not Heard the Good News

Most would agree that people are not Christians in many parts of the world today because access to the Gospel has been forbidden or closed to those areas. The people cannot believe because they cannot hear the good news. God has chosen the *means* of salvation to be the preaching of the Gospel. Paul said, "I am not ashamed of the gospel, because it is the power of God for the salvation of everyone who believes" (Rom. 1:16). If healing is part of the Gospel, should it then follow that the hearing of the Gospel must be present before people can be divinely healed? Faith comes by hearing, and faith is a key ingredient for healing. People need to hear the message of healing to increase their faith.

Sometimes People Are Not Healed Because They Do Not Have Faith for Healing

This is a hard statement, but if we look at the evidence, it is true. Sometimes people do not have faith in God as a healer. Maybe they have been taught that God is removed from our situations and does not heal today. They may even be Christians and on their way to heaven, but they have not been taught to have faith for healing. Also, some allow experiences of the past to hinder their ability to believe for the present. Maybe a loved one died from a disease and was not healed, resulting in a surviving family member losing faith for his healing. Or maybe the sick person has no confidence in the person who is ministering healing to him. This happened in Nazareth when Jesus visited. Not many people were healed because of the *lack of faith*. They could not believe that Jesus was sent from God and did not even venture out to allow Him to heal them.

Sometimes People Are Not Healed Because of Disobedience

Many times in Scripture the person needing healing was commanded to do something. Healing was a result of his faith, the Lord's power, and this individual's obedience to Jesus' command. What if any one of these three elements was missing? I would dare say that healing would not have occurred. If faith is not present—therefore, hindering the release of God's power and the obedience of the person in need of healing—it is probably safe to say that healing will not happen. Three ingredients should be present for healing to occur—faith, the Lord's power, and obedience to the Lord's commands. If only one of these three elements is not present, healing may not occur. For example, if only the obedience of the person in need of a healing is absent—i.e. God has commanded a person to do something and he does not do it—healing may not happen.

There was a story told by R.W. Schambach years ago. He traveled with A.A. Allen and shared how one night a lady, who could not see out of one eye, came forward for healing. Brother Allen prayed for her and nothing happened. He sensed that something was wrong and told the lady to go and do what God had told her to do and to not come back until she had obeyed. Brother Schambach said the lady returned on another night and got in line for healing. When she reached A.A. Allen, he asked her if she had obeyed. She said she had not, and Allen refused to pray for her. Eventually, after Allen refused to pray for the lady night after night, Schambach said he saw this woman walk to the side of the altar area, place her hands on her hips, and say, "Alright, God, I'll pay my tithes." Schambach said that when the lady said those words, her eye popped open and she could see. Obedience resulted in a miracle.

Sometimes People Are Not Healed Because It's Their Time to Die

Unless Jesus returns, every living person will die at some time. Many times we have prayed for healing when a person is ready to die. I know some would argue that just because there is a time appointed for every person to die, this doesn't mean they have to die of sickness and disease. I understand this argument, but I must confess that I have prayed for many wonderful Christian believers who have died from various diseases and sicknesses. I believe, in such a case as this, that we can say these were actually healed when they left their body. They were not denied.

I want us to be careful here, however. There may be a tendency to use this point as an excuse for not believing in healing. Some may refuse to believe for healing because they believe a particular sickness is *God's will.* But Scripture is clear that God's will is healing—this is the *revealed* will of God to us. If someone is going to die, we don't usually know that. Sometimes God may speak to us as we pray and tell us that this person is going to die, but unless God speaks that to me, I am going to pray the revealed will of God—to heal the sick.

Sometimes People Aren't Healed Because Prayer Was Misdirected

Sometimes a sickness is caused by a demonic spirit. Let us make note of the following verses:

> *Now He was teaching in one of the synagogues on the Sabbath. ¹¹ And behold, there was a woman who had a spirit of infirmity eighteen years, and was bent over and could in no way raise herself up. ¹²But when Jesus saw her, He called her to Him and said to her, "Woman, you are loosed from your infirmity."* (LUKE 13:10-12 NKJV)

It is obvious that the cause of this woman's sickness was a "spirit of infirmity." Jesus commanded the woman to be loosed from this, and she was healed. Often people do not discern the root causes of a sickness. If a spirit is present, it must be cast out.

This discussion leads to another aspect of the biblical basis for healing. Is healing part of the covenant we have with God according the New Testament? Many use the Scripture passage found in Isaiah 53:5 as proof that the ministry of Jesus, along with the covenant He inaugurated, included healing as much as it did salvation for the soul: "But He was pierced for our transgressions, He was crushed for our iniquities; the punishment that brought us peace was upon Him, and by His wounds we are healed."

It has been accepted in Pentecostal and Charismatic circles for years that the *healing* spoken of here refers to *bodily* healing as well as *spiritual* healing. If we follow the logic of bodily healing in the Atonement, we will arrive at this conclusion: All who come to God in faith *will* be healed because it is provided in the Atonement just as salvation is provided in the Atonement. *Just as* salvation is received by faith as part of the rights and privileges of the believer, healing can be received as part of the rights and privileges of the believer.

Is healing part of the covenant? Do we always receive all of the benefits of the covenant in this life? I would have to answer, "Yes," to the first question and, "No," to the second. Yes, I believe healing is a part of the covenant blessing. However, some do not receive the fullness of the covenant blessing in this life. Why? I will refer you back to the statements on why some do not receive healing. I believe healing is available to all based on the covenant of God secured through Jesus' death on the cross.

Endnotes

95 T. L. Osborn, *Healing & God's Will*, [http://jesus-is-lord.albertarose. org/TLOsborn.htm]. Accessed September 2012.

chapter 8

HOLINESS—
A Christian's Calling

In Jesus, the holy one of God who makes us holy, a divine humility was the secret of his life and his death and his exaltation; the one infallible test of our holiness will be the humility before God and men which marks us. Humility is the bloom and the beauty of holiness.[96]
—Andrew Murray

Holiness is the everyday business of every Christian. It evidences itself in the decisions we make and the things we do, hour by hour, day by day.[97]
—Charles W. Colson

One aspect of living the Christian life that has received considerable attention in the past, though not as much attention in the contemporary church, is holiness—which is simply living a righteous and godly life. Actually the term *holiness* is akin to the term *sanctification*. Both expressions derive from the same Greek root word *hagios*. When we accept Jesus as

Savior and Lord, He transforms our life. The process of salvation goes something like this: Firstly, we respond to the call of God and repent, this is the result of faith that has arisen in our heart. God then justifies us (declares us righteous and just). He then begins in us the process of sanctification, and we are sealed by the Holy Spirit as His. Of course, we must persevere until the end, at which time He will receive us to Himself—with glorification aptly describing this occasion.

THE CALL TO HOLINESS

After becoming a Christian, God is ever present to help us live a victorious life. He provides the Holy Spirit to help us overcome temptations and to live a holy life. Sanctification means that we have been "set apart"[98] for God and His service. It also means that we have been "set apart" from sin. So, we can think of this experience as having both a positive and a negative aspect.

The children of Israel were called to be holy. God declares as much over them in Exodus 19:6, when He says, "'You will be for Me a kingdom of priests and a holy nation.' These are the words you [Moses] are to speak to the Israelites."

Holiness, in fact, was to be a distinguishing characteristic of the people of Israel. They were God's people and they would stand out as different, peculiar, and even a bit strange among the nations. God had called them to be holy because He is holy, as Leviticus 11:44-45 so very clearly states: "I am the Lord your God; consecrate yourselves and be holy, because I am holy. Do not make yourselves unclean by any creature that moves about on the ground. I am the Lord who brought you up out of Egypt to be your God; therefore be holy, because I am holy."

The command of holiness was no less emphasized in the New Testament. Jesus prayed for the sanctification of His disciples: "Sanctify them by the truth; Your word is truth" (John 17:17).

Paul prayed for the church in Thessalonica that they would be sanctified: "May God Himself, the God of peace, sanctify you through and through. May your whole spirit, soul and body be kept blameless at the coming of our Lord Jesus Christ" (1 Thess. 5:23).

To be holy, like God, is the *will* of God. In 1 Thessalonians 4:3, we read, "It is God's will that you should be sanctified: that you should avoid sexual immorality." This may seem overwhelming to us, but there is good news: We are not left to our own strength to live holy; we have been united with Christ through the power of the Holy Spirit. Now the life of God is living in us, and He will give us the power to live holy. We are not left alone in the universe. We are not left exposed to the power of sin and evil. Christ lives in us and "greater is He that is in you, than He that is in the world" (1 John 4:4 KJV)

The key to walking in holiness is to stay in relationship with God, who is the source of our holiness. We are holy *because* He is holy. Yet, this does not mean that we do nothing to move ourselves toward holiness and righteous. We must, and we are commanded, to pursue holiness and to put to death the evil that wrestles against us.

> *Since, then, you have been raised with Christ,* **set your hearts on things above,** *where Christ is seated at the right hand of God.* **Set your minds on things above,** *not on earthly things. For you died, and your life is now hidden with Christ in God. When Christ, who is your life, appears, then you also will appear with Him in glory. Put to death, therefore, whatever belongs to your earthly nature: sexual immorality, impurity, lust, evil desires and greed, which is idolatry. Because of these, the wrath of God is coming. You used to walk in these ways, in the life you once lived.* **But now you must rid yourselves of all such things as these:** *anger, rage, malice, slander, and filthy language from your lips. Do not lie to each other, since you have taken off your old self with its practices and have put on the new self, which is being renewed in knowledge in the image of its Creator. Here there is no Greek or Jew, circumcised or uncircumcised, barbarian, Scythian, slave or free, but Christ is all, and is in all.*
> (COLOSSIANS 3:1-11, EMPHASIS ADDED)

In this passage, notice the constant cause and effect relationships. "**Since** . . . you have been raised with Christ," (cause), then ". . . **set** your hearts on things above," "put to death . . . whatever belongs to your earthly nature" (effects). "**Do not** lie to each other," (effects), ". . . **since** you have taken off your old self with its practices and have put on the new self, which is being renewed in knowledge in the image of its Creator" (cause). Our holiness is based and grounded in God's holiness. Because of His work on the Cross, we can live holy.

HOW ARE WE SANCTIFIED?

We have seen that God calls us to holiness but does not leave us to our own strength to attain such. He participates in this, helping us and infusing us with His power and ability. However, this does not mean that we do not play a part in the sanctification process. Our calling to be holy means we have a command and responsibility in the process. The Bible gives us several means or ways to holiness.

Offer Yourself to God

> *Do not offer the parts of your body to sin, as instruments of wickedness, but rather offer yourselves to God, as those whohave been brought from death to life; and offer the parts of your body to Him as instruments of righteousness.*
> (ROMANS 6:13, SEE ALSO ROMANS 12:1)

The NIV, in this particular Scripture reference, uses the expression, "offer yourselves to God," whereas the

NKJV translates this as, "present yourselves to God." The idea is one of yielding, offering, or presenting one's mind and heart to God. This implies making a conscious choice each day to yield ourselves to God as His servants. Though we are a Christian by virtue of the work God has performed in our heart, we must also make a decision to walk in the way of Christ every day. This is a positive and even passive way of walking in holiness—positive and passive in that God is doing the work and we are positioned in a receiving mode.

Put to Death the Old Ways

> For if you live according to the sinful nature, you will die; but if by the Spirit you put to death the misdeeds of the body, you will live. (ROMANS 8:13)

Notice how *The Message Bible* very interestingly renders this verse:

> So don't you see that we don't owe this old do-it-yourself life one red cent. There's nothing in it for us, nothing at all. The best thing to do is give it a decent burial and get on with your new life. God's Spirit beckons. There are things to do and places to go! (ROMANS 8:12-14)

This is how we should treat the sinful nature—*give it a decent burial and get on with our new life!* We should determine that we are not going to allow the old sinful patterns to rule our life any longer, that we are a new creature and are going to join the Spirit of God within us and walk in the newness of life. This means of sanctification is an active one. We must take an active role in our walk of holiness. There are numerous Scriptures which admonish us to live holy, only a few of which are as follows:

Make every effort to live in peace with all men and to be holy; without holiness no one will see the Lord. (HEBREWS 12:14)

It is God's will that you should be sanctified: that you should avoid sexual immorality; that each of you should learn to control his own body in a way that is holy and honorable, not in passionate lust like the heathen, who do not know God; and that in this matter no one should wrong his brother or take advantage of him. The Lord will punish men for all such sins, as we have already told you and warned you. For God did not call us to be impure, but to live a holy life. (1 THESSALONIANS 4:3-7)

Do not be yoked together with unbelievers. For what do righteousness and wickedness have in common? Or what fellowship can light have with darkness? (2 CORINTHIANS 6:14)

For this very reason, make every effort to add to your faith goodness; and to goodness, knowledge; and to knowledge, self-control; and to self-control, perseverance; and to perseverance, godliness; and to godliness, brotherly kindness; and to brotherly kindness, love. For if you possess these qualities in increasing measure, they will keep you from being ineffective and unproductive in your knowledge of our Lord Jesus Christ. But if anyone does not have them, he is nearsighted and blind,and has forgotten that he has been cleansed from his past sins. (2 PETER 1:5-9)

Get into the Bible

The Bible plays a major role in our sanctification. As we read the Bible on a regular basis, we will be changed—because *"faith comes from hearing the message, and the message is heard through the Word of Christ"* (Romans 10:17). We must be reading or listening to the words of faith before we can grow in faith. In fact, Jesus prayed for His disciples that the Father would "sanctify them by the truth; Your word is truth" (John 17:17). The Word of God has the power to cleanse and sanctify us—may we take full advantage of it.

Pray

We must not overlook the importance of prayer in the process of sanctification. Though the subject of prayer has been dealt with in-depth in a previous chapter, we will make mention that this is a spiritual discipline that plays a major role in our walk of holiness. Paul told the Ephesians, "Pray in the Spirit on *all* occasions with all kinds of prayers and requests. With this in mind, be alert and always keep on praying for all the saints" (Eph. 6:18, emphasis added).

Worship God

Worship is yet another subject dealt with in detail in another chapter of this book—one to come. However, it is important at this time to point out the significant role this discipline plays in our sanctification and progression in holiness. John Piper said,

> Missions is not the ultimate goal of the Church. Worship is. Missions exists because worship doesn't. Worship is ultimate, not missions, because God is ultimate, not man. When this age is over, and the countless millions of the redeemed fall on their faces before the throne of God, missions will be no more. It is a temporary necessity. But worship abides forever.
>
> Worship, therefore, is the fuel and goal of missions. It's the goal of missions because in missions we simply aim to bring the nations into the white hot enjoyment of God's glory. The goal of missions is the gladness of the peoples in the greatness of God. "The Lord reigns; let the earth rejoice; let the many coastlands be glad!" (Ps. 97:1). "Let the peoples praise thee, O God; let all the peoples praise thee! Let the nations be glad and sing for joy!" (PSALM 67:3-4).[99]

The goal of our lives should be to worship God. Notice that does not just mean singing and raising our hands. Worship is a lifestyle. It is acknowledging God as the Lord of the universe and submitting ourselves to Him. The Westminster Shorter Catechism's first question is:

"What is the chief end of man?" And the answer is: "Man's chief end is to glorify God, and to enjoy Him forever."[100]

We must take time to worship God. We must take time to be with Him regularly. We must take time to reflect and meditate on God's Word and on His goodness.

Attend Church

Attending church is one of the simplest means to holiness. It is vitally important that we attend church. When we do so, we join our faith with those gathered with us. There is a special atmosphere present when many different believers come together for the sole purpose of worshipping God.

The church does not consist of the building, chairs, and carpet, but rather the people of God who worship together. There we will be encouraged to live another week for God. There we will worship with others of like faith. There we will hear the Word preached, which alone has the message of salvation. There we can find prayer support from others. May we prioritize our life and make attending church a must, as Hebrews 10:24-25 strongly encourages us to do: "And let us consider how we may spur one another on toward love and good deeds. Let us not give up meeting together, as some are in the habit of doing, but let us encourage one another—and all the more as you see the Day approaching."

Witness

Witnessing, as well, is a matter of focus in another chapter of this volume. Yet, this discipline is also a part of the daily walk of holiness to which we are called. Jesus taught us to be salt and light in the world. We are to be an influence in the world. We are not to hide our witness or compromise our witness. We are to be the light of the world, which is in darkness, so its inhabitants may see the way home.

Jesus taught us to "go and make disciples of all nations" (Matt. 28:19). The emphasis here is on *going* and *making*. These two verbs teach us a lot about the public witness we are to have for Christ. We are to go—go to those who haven't heard the Good News, go to those who need help, go to anyone who is accepting of our witness. Next, we are to make them. Make them what? We are to make them disciples. This comes about by teaching and witness through words and actions. In the ancient world, disciples were made by following a master, listening to his teaching, and imitating his lifestyle. We should imitate the life of Jesus so others can follow us. This is why Paul could say to the Corinthians, "Even though you have ten thousand guardians in Christ, you do not have many fathers, for in Christ Jesus I became your father through the gospel. Therefore I urge you to imitate me" (1 Cor. 4:15-16).

In considering all of the ingredients that have been given for growth in holiness, there are no shortcuts to experiencing such. There is no quick fix. Growth in holiness is just that—*growth*. A saying that for many years has helped me keep mindful of the difference between gifts of the Spirit and fruit of the Spirit is: *Gifts flow; fruit grows.* Gifts can flow through us as God wills, but the fruit of the Spirit takes time to find root and produce in our lives.

DIFFERENT VIEWS OF SANCTIFICATION

There have been many different views of sanctification in the past. It is important to understand positions on this subject that have been accepted throughout history. Two quite different views in this regard can be illustrated in a very simplistic way.

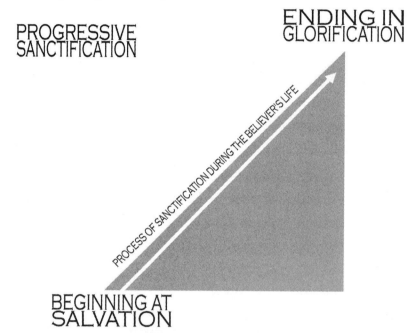

Progressive sanctification implies that God begins the process of sanctification in one's heart when that person repents and turns to Him. This process will then continue throughout the believer's life. It will not even end at death, but will rather do so when Jesus returns and resurrects the dead, presenting the resurrected believers with new bodies. Then the believer will be *glorified*.

Wesleyan "Entire Sanctification"

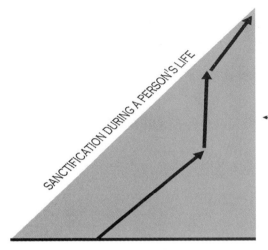

Entire Sanctification
AT ONE MOMENT!

John Wesley was an Anglican minister in the 1700s who started a movement that eventually became the Methodist Church. He was a gifted organizer, writer, and preacher. The theory of sanctification that he developed is often referred to as "perfect love." In brief, he believed a person could receive perfect love, or entire sanctification, in this life. This led his followers to ardently strive toward holiness. His view of sanctification is represented as progressive but with a major "leap" happening at the point of receiving the experience of entire sanctification.[101] The early Pentecostals, for the most part, held to this view of sanctification because they were birthed out of the Holiness movement which was a direct descendent of Wesleyanism.[102]

❈ *Synthesis View of Sanctification*

A mix of the two aforementioned sanctification views will now be offered. I believe sanctification is progressive. It must begin at conversion to Christ. However, there is growth in holiness and sanctification—giving it its progressive aspect. But what about experiences? What about the times when the Holy Spirit touches us, and we move up a little faster, or so it seems? Every touch of the Holy Spirit should affect our life in a sanctifying way. Thus, our progression in holiness could show many little surges upward. This should encourage us to keep pressing forward toward holiness and to believe God for more. This "Synthesis View of Sanctification" can be illustrated as shown as follows.

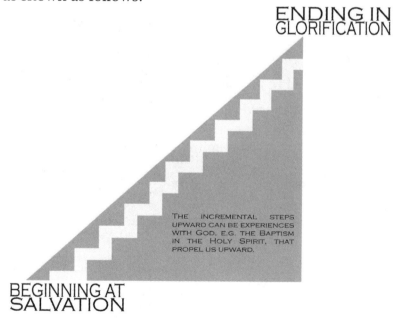

ENDING IN GLORIFICATION

THE INCREMENTAL STEPS UPWARD CAN BE EXPERIENCES WITH GOD, E.G. THE BAPTISM IN THE HOLY SPIRIT, THAT PROPEL US UPWARD.

BEGINNING AT SALVATION

WHAT ABOUT THE LAW?

One final issue needs to be addressed before leaving this subject of "Holiness—A Christian's Calling." As Christians, are we supposed to obey the Old Testament law? With there being so many different laws and commands in the Old Testament, how can a believer possibly fulfill all of them?

Basically, there were two divisions of the law in the Old Testament. Firstly, there was the moral law of God. That is, God revealed to Israel His will which was based on His character—holiness. Secondly, God instituted certain ways to worship Him and to atone for sin. This is called the ceremonial law. As Christians, we should be concerned with how these laws are treated in the New Testament.

Jesus mentioned the commandments of God and said that He did not come to destroy the law "but to fulfill" it (Matt. 5:17) it. He reiterated much of the Ten Commandments in His teaching. But in the book of Acts, when the apostles were faced with the question of whether the Gentiles coming into the church were to obey the Jewish ceremonial law, the answer was, "No." They were commanded to abstain from sexual immorality and to avoid meat sacrificed to idols only. From this we can conclude that the dietary laws, festivals, and sacrifices of the Old Testament have passed away (or been fulfilled) in

Christ. Yet, the moral law stands intact as the will of God for His people. What does this mean? This means we should obey the Ten Commandments. We must realize that our salvation does not come through obeying the law but through faith in Christ. But, faith in Christ is *manifested* by our desire to keep the moral law of God.

Sanctification changes our heart and desires toward God. Through God's sanctifying power, we take joy in doing good and obeying God's commands, "for it is God who works in you to will and to act according to His good purpose" (Phil. 2:13).

Endnotes

[96] Andrew Murray, *Humility: The Journey Toward Holiness* (Minneapolis: Bethany House, 2001) Chapter 7.

[97] Charles W. Colson, *Loving God* (Grand Rapids: Zondervan, 1983), 131.

[98] BAGD, s.v. "hagiadzo."

[99] John Piper, *Let the Nations Be Glad! The Supremacy of God in Missions*, 2nd ed. (Grand Rapids: Baker, 2003).

[100] Westminster Shorter Catechism, [http://www.creeds.net/Westminster/shorter_catechism.html]. Accessed 2013.

[101] See John Wesley, *A Plain Account of Christian Perfection in Readings in Christian Theology: The New Life*, vol. 3, ed. Millard J. Erickson (Grand Rapids: Baker, 1979), 159-167.

[102] See Vinson Synan, *The Holiness-Pentecostal Movement* (Grand Rapids: Eerdmans, 1972).

chapter 9

WORSHIP— A Christian's Response

Oh, give thanks to the LORD! Call upon His name; Make known His deeds among the peoples! (PSALM 105:1 NKJV)

Let them praise His name with the dance; let them sing praises to Him with the timbrel and harp. (PSALM 149:3 NKJV)

A natural response to receiving the gift of a new life is to return thanks to God. The natural response to God for all that He has done is to thank Him and worship Him. Our focus in this volume has now come to what it means to worship God. We use the term praise very often when we want to brag on someone. Well, the Bible uses this word praise frequently, as well.

THANKSGIVING

At the outset, there is another term that is important in Scripture and that needs to be brought into our discussion—*thanksgiving.* What does it mean to give thanks? The apostle Paul told the Thessalonians to "give thanks in all circumstances, for this is God's will for you in Christ Jesus" (1 Thess. 5:18). The term used here for thanksgiving is *euchariste.* The root for this word is *cara,* which is joy. Of course, *charis* takes on the meaning of "what delights."[103] Thanksgiving, then, is a *response* for something given. It includes the emotion of the event, as well, which is joy. Thanksgiving becomes a delight in our hearts for the grace of God given to us.

Notice Paul said "in all circumstances." The delight we have in response to God's gift of grace to us sustains us in all types of situations. If we are having a good day, we should be thankful. If we are having a bad day, we should be thankful. We don't have to be thankful *for* the bad day but thankful *in* the bad day. We don't have to pretend or put on a front and try to make the world think we are some superhuman who gives thanks and shouts and dances because we are going through a tough time. On the other hand, we need to get the right perspective, the right focus. In the midst of our trials, we should give thanks *to God.* Why? He is the One who rules heaven and earth, and He is the only One who can truly bring deliverance to us *in* the midst of our situation. One of the most powerful tools we can have as a Christian is the attitude of thankfulness. Let us begin to develop thankfulness every day, and it will help us when attacks come.

Thanksgiving Is an Attitude

Thanksgiving is not just an act but an *attitude*. We are to develop an attitude of thankfulness. If we are born again, here are some things to be thankful for: God created us, sent His Son to die for us, rescued us from despair, cleansed us from sin, broke the power of sin from our life, reserved for us an eternity with Him, endowed us with power and authority over Satan, and bestowed spiritual gifts to us. These are but a few things He has done for us. Therefore, we should be thankful at all times. If we are struggling with this, we should work to cultivate an attitude of thankfulness. We may have to write down on paper some things we are thankful for and then let the blessings soak in for a while as we look at what God has given us in life that is worthy of thanksgiving.

We may ask, "How do I cultivate an attitude of thankfulness when everything is falling apart in my life?" I believe the answer is to first understand the calling power of God. We are in the kingdom of God, because He called us. God valued us so much that He called us into His kingdom. This entire event was for something. We have a destiny, a divine calling, a purpose. God has placed us in His kingdom for a specific reason. This is our hour and our time. We must not let this time pass us by while we walk in an attitude of unthankfulness.

Let us consider the following Scriptures concerning our calling and allow them to take hold in our thinking:

*And you also are among those who are called **to belong to Jesus Christ**. To all in Rome who are loved by God and called **to be saints**.* (ROMANS 1:6-7, EMPHASIS ADDED)

*And we know that **in all things God works for the good** of those who love Him, who have been called according to His purpose.* (ROMANS 8:28, EMPHASIS ADDED)

*To the church of God in Corinth, to those sanctified in Christ Jesus and called **to be holy**, . . .* (1 CORINTHIANS 1:2, EMPHASIS ADDED)

*But to those whom God has called, both Jews and Greeks, **Christ the power of God and the wisdom of God**.* (1 CORINTHIANS 1:24, EMPHASIS ADDED)

*Jude, a servant of Jesus Christ and a brother of James, To those who have been called, **who are loved** by God the Father **and kept** by Jesus Christ . . .* (JUDE 1, EMPHASIS ADDED)

*You, my brothers, were called **to be free** . . .* (GALATIANS 5:13, EMPHASIS ADDED)

*Let the peace of Christ rule in your hearts, since as members of one body you were called **to peace**.* (COLOSSIANS 3:15, EMPHASIS ADDED)

*Fight the good fight of the faith. Take hold of the **eternal life to which you were called** when you made your good confession in the presence of many witnesses.* (1 TIMOTHY 6:12, EMPHASIS ADDED)

*For this reason Christ is the mediator of a new covenant, that those who are called **may receive the promised eternal inheritance**—now that He has died as a ransom to set them free from the sins committed under the first covenant.* (HEBREWS 9:15, EMPHASIS ADDED)

*Do not repay evil with evil or insult with insult, but with blessing, because to this you were called **so that you may inherit a blessing**.* (1 PETER 3:9, EMPHASIS ADDED)

Let us think on these passages for days to come. How blessed we are to be one of the chosen. We are loaded down with the favor of God.

The process of God calling us into His kingdom *should* produce a serious thankfulness in our hearts. What can deter us from pursuing God if we know that we are the called? Being the called of God gives us enough reason to be eternally grateful. Even in Revelation, the twenty-four elders and creatures around the throne sang a new song, "You are worthy to take the scroll and to open its seals, because you were slain, and with your blood you purchased men for God from every tribe and language and people and nation. You have made them to be a kingdom of priests to serve our God, and they will reign on the earth" (Rev. 5:9-10). This thankfulness will be eternal. Throughout the ages of eternity, our hearts will be filled with thankfulness over the Son of God who came to save sinners such as you and I.

Repulsive would be an apt descriptor for how it would feel to be in the presence of someone who is unthankful, especially if that person is a Christian. Allowance could possibly be made for unthankfulness coming from someone who has not yet had the light of the Gospel revealed to them—but not from a Christian. The list of aforementioned Scriptures provides reasons enough to make any believer rejoice. A Christian who has a rotten attitude and is unthankful, no doubt, has gotten off course. He has stopped looking at his blessing and started focusing on his circumstances. By giving thanks, we focus our minds and hearts on the blessing of being called by God instead of the present circumstances. Let us develop an attitude of thankfulness—this is the first step in being a true worshipper of God.

PRAISE

Thankfulness is the *attitude* that serves as the basis for our heart's pursuit of God. Praise is the *action*. Praise is an action that expresses the *attitude* of our heart toward God. If we don't have the right attitude, the action will be off base or insincere. On the other hand, if we don't exhibit the action, the attitude will remain dormant without expression. We need both the proper attitude and the proper action toward God.

OLD TESTAMENT TERMS

In the Scriptures, *praise* is a term that appears frequently in the Old Testament, especially in the Psalms. Two major terms used in the Old Testament for praise are *halal*[104] and *tehillah*.[105]

The Hebrew term *halal* conveys the meaning "to be clear, usually of color; to make a show; to boast; foolish; rave; to celebrate."[106] The term actually represents "the giving off of light by celestial bodies." It means "to be sincerely and deeply thankful for and/or satisfied in lauding a superior quality(ies) or great, great act(s) of the object."[107] About one-third of the uses of the term *halal* in the Old Testament appear in the Psalms. "The largest number of these are imperative summons to praise. The frequency and mood emphasizes the necessity of this action."[108] The term is linked closely with Israel's corporate praise and is used in the context of faith and joy. In Psalm 109:30, we see expressed both the congregational aspect of praise and the lifting up of one's voice: "With my mouth I will greatly extol the Lord; in the great throng I will praise Him."

The term *tehillah* means "a laudation" or "hymn." It "represents the results of halal as well as divine acts which merit that activity."[109] We find this expressed in the following Scripture verse: "God came from Teman, the Holy One from Mount Paran. 'Selah' His glory covered the heavens and His praise filled the earth" (Hab. 3:3).

NEW TESTAMENT TERMS

In the New Testament, several terms are used for praise. One such term is *eulogeo*, meaning to "speak well of." This term also carries the meaning of blessing—to bless others or God.[110] One such example of this in Scripture is: "In a loud voice they sang: 'Worthy is the Lamb, who was slain, to receive power and wealth and wisdom and strength and honor and glory and praise'" (Revelation 5:12; cf. Luke 1:64).

A second New Testament term for praise is *aineo*. The term *aineo* simply means "to praise," and is reserved for God. This word appears eight times in the New Testament and appears as a "joyful praise of God in hymn or prayer by individuals (Luke 2:20; Acts 3:8-9), a group (Luke 19:37), the community (Acts 2:47; Rev. 19:5), or angels (Luke 2:13).[111]

A third term for praise in the New Testament is *epaineo*, which also simply carries the meaning of "to give praise to." The noun form, *epainos*, can be used in giving praise, approval or recognition to men and to God.[112]

A final term to consider is *humneo*, which carries the meaning of singing praise to God.[113] Praise is expressed in the early Christian community in song form. God's story of salvation is conveyed in song forms of praise. (Acts 16:25; Hebrews 2:12.)

PRAISING GOD FOR HIS QUALITIES

We are to praise God for who He is and for His mighty acts. Our duty to praise Him is beautifully detailed in Psalm 150 ESV:

> Praise the Lord!
> Praise God in His sanctuary; praise Him in His mighty heavens!
>
> Praise Him for His mighty deeds; praise Him according to His excellent greatness!
>
> Praise Him with the trumpet sound; praise Him with the lute and harp!
>
> Praise Him with tambourine and dance; praise Him with strings and pipe!
> Praise Him with sounding cymbals; praise Him with loud clashing cymbals!
>
> Let everything that has breath praise the Lord!
> Praise the Lord!

In the first line, this psalm admonishes us to praise in His sanctuary, that is, with others in the atmosphere of the congregation's worship. Also, we are admonished to praise Him in the realm of His power, which is the entire universe. When we praise God, our praise extends from the local sanctuary to the realm of the heavens, the expanse of the universe. When we praise God, our praise lifts beyond our temporal surroundings; it rises to the atmosphere of God.

In the second line, we are admonished to praise God for His mighty deeds. Our praise is to focus upon God's mighty deeds, His powerful acts, His creation and governance of the universe. Coupled with this is reflection upon God's mighty power—as in, His excellent greatness. Only God, who is all-wise, all-powerful and all-knowing, could call into existence a world such as the one we live in with its intricacies and detailed design. This should cause us to raise our hands and give Him praise.

In the third, fourth, and fifth lines, music instruments and dancing are associated with praising God. In essence, praise to God involves the emotions as well as the intellect. Let us focus for a moment on the phrase "according to His excellent greatness." The true meaning of praise is when we go beyond our surroundings and beyond just giving thanks for things God has done or will do. Praise reaches higher when we praise God for who He is. He is excellent in His greatness. Theologians have written through the centuries about the characteristics of God or His attributes. This is a good place to make note of a few of the attributes of God that should give us reason to praise Him.

God Is Spirit

We limit our thinking about God when we confine Him to space and time. God is Spirit; He is beyond space and time. He is not made of matter as we know things to be in this world.[114] He cannot rust or corrupt; He will not suffer the effects that all created things suffer. He cannot die; He will not age. He is eternal because He is Spirit, as John 4:24 so clearly states, "God is Spirit, and His worshippers must worship Him in spirit and in truth."

God Is Invisible

We cannot see God. We can only see of Him what He allows us to. This is one reason why the saints of old longed for the end of life when they would see God. This was called the beatific vision. First Timothy 1:17 tells us, "Now to the King eternal, immortal, invisible, the only God, be honor and glory for ever and ever. Amen."

God Is All-Knowing

God is the only one perfect in knowledge. We know in part and prophesy in part, but God knows everything immediately and fully. There is no part of our lives that goes unseen or unknown by God. There is no need or trial we face that God doesn't know about.

> *The Spirit searches all things even the deep things of God.* (1 CORINTHIANS 2:10)

> *O Lord, you have searched me and you know me.* (PSALM 139:1)

God Is All-Wise

God's wisdom goes beyond His knowledge of all things. In His wisdom, He makes all the right choices.

Every decision or decree of His is perfect and all-wise. This gives us reason to pause and reflect and be reminded that God is worthy to be praised.

> *To the only wise God be glory forever through Jesus Christ! Amen.* (ROMANS 16:27)

> *How many are Your works, O Lord! In wisdom You made them all; the earth is full of Your creatures.* (PSALM 104:24)

God Is Truthful

God is the only *true* God. All other gods or things worshipped fall short of the God of Israel. God is to be praised, because He is God *period*. God is total truth, as well. All of His actions are true. There is no lying or deceit in Him. This also means that God is ultimately faithful. He cannot fail in His promises. (Numbers 23:19.)

> *"Now this is eternal life: that they may know You, the only true God, and Jesus Christ, whom You have sent."* (JOHN 17:3)

> *He is the Rock, His works are perfect, and all His ways are just* ... (DEUTERONOMY 32:4)

God Is Good

Good is "what God approves."[115] He is the ultimate standard of good. All of His creation is "good." "'Why do you call me good?' Jesus answered. 'No one is good— except God alone'" (Luke 18:19).

God Is Love

God's character is love, as 1 John 4:8 so clearly states, "Whoever does not love does not know God, because God is love." And the ultimate expression of God's love was in sending Jesus to mankind. In fact, Jesus described it as "no greater love."[116]

God Is Merciful

God is full of mercy. Mercy is the love of God expressed to someone who cannot help himself. Thank God that His mercies are new every morning; they never wear out.

> *Remember, O Lord, Your great mercy and love for they are from of old.* (PSALM 25:6)

God Is Holy

God's character is holy, sanctified, set apart. Nothing about God is common or profane. No sin can stand before Him without justice being executed. When we touch God, we touch His holiness and it transforms our very being. When Isaiah saw the Lord in his inaugural vision, the first thing that hit him hard was his own sinfulness. A proper vision of God should cause us to have a realistic view of ourselves. Isaiah proclaimed, "Holy, holy, holy is the Lord Almighty" (Isa. 6:3).

God Is Peace

He is Jehovah-Shalom, the God of Peace. When we touch God, we touch pure peace. No wonder Jesus could step out on the bow of the ship in the midst of a violent storm and simply say, "Peace, be still" (Mark 4:39 KJV). He is the God of peace. Paul, in Colossians 3:15, tells us, "Let the peace of Christ rule in your hearts, since as members of one body you were called to peace."

God Is Righteousness

Everything about God is correct, true, and honest. He is righteousness. We never have to worry about the correctness of His judgments or decisions, as the psalmist so strongly states, "Righteous are You, O Lord, and Your laws are right" (Ps. 119:137).

God Is All-Powerful

God has all power and authority. The only authority the Devil or mankind has is that which has been granted him or them based upon God's sovereignty. "When Abraham was ninety-nine years old, the Lord appeared to him and said, 'I am God Almighty; walk before Me and be blameless'" (Gen. 17:1).

God Is Perfect

There are no imperfections in God. He is pure, holy, and perfect. Our goal, as believers, is to conform to His perfection. In the New Testament, this takes the sense of being mature or growing into such a place of being or existence. Will we ever reach the state of perfection? Obviously not, at least not in our current bodies, but it is a goal for which we strive. "Be perfect, therefore, as your heavenly Father is perfect" (Matt. 5:48).

God Is Beautiful

This is one of the most endearing of God's attributes, because it relates to us on an intimate basis. When we think of beauty in our contemporary world, we think of glamour or Hollywood. But God is *truly* beautiful. He is the perfection of beauty that we should desire. Art, in ancient times, was looked upon as representing something heavenly, ideal. Now, unfortunately, some art forms have stooped to all-time lows, and the purpose of art in some circles is to display anything that the artist dreams up, even if without moral boundaries. But true art is to reflect true beauty. God is the ideal of true beauty.

It is no wonder that the psalmist David requested, "One thing I ask of the Lord, this is what I seek; that I may dwell in the house of the Lord all the days of my life, to gaze upon the beauty of the Lord and to seek Him in His temple" (Ps. 27:4).

God Is Glory

The Hebrew sense of the term *glory* denotes "heaviness."[117] There is weightiness to the glory of God. His glory is His renown, His fame. This is so strong when it comes to God that it is tangible. When Isaiah saw God in his vision, he saw angelic creatures crying, "The whole earth is full of His glory" (Isa. 6:3). He also saw God's train filling the temple. In ancient times an emperor's train represented his fame or battles won. God has such glory that His train *filled* the temple. When the priests dedicated the Tabernacle in the Old Testament, the glory came into the structure to the extent that the priests could no longer minister. It was tangible. In Exodus 15:11, we read: "Who among the gods is like You, O Lord? Who is like You—majestic in holiness, awesome in glory, working wonders?"

All of the aforementioned are reasons to praise God. We should have no reason or excuse for falling short in our praises to Him. If nothing is going right in our life, we still have a reason to praise God. If we get so low that we feel as though God has done nothing for us, we just need to reread the list of His characteristics and praise Him just for who He is.

CREATED TO WORSHIP

Scripture makes it very clear that we were created to worship. In beginning our study of praise, we first asked what praise is. Now we turn to an anthropological view of such. What is man's role in praise?

God created man and woman as spiritual beings. Not only do we have flesh and blood, but we also are spiritual. But it is a spirit in man, and the breath of the Almighty gives them understanding. (Job 32:8 NASB)

> *The spirit of man is the lamp of the Lord, searching all the innermost parts of his being.* (PROVERBS 20:27 NASB)

> *Then the dust will return to the earth as it was, and the spirit will return to God who gave it.* (ECCLESIASTES 12:7 NASB)

> *They went on stoning Stephen as he called on the Lord and said, "Lord Jesus, receive my spirit!"* (ACTS 7:59 NASB)

> *For just as the body without the spirit is dead, so also faith without works is dead.* (JAMES 2:26 NASB)

As a spiritual being, man longs to connect with the God who created him. The born again person longs to worship God even if he doesn't know how. Man's role in praise is to offer up praise and worship to God. In this act man is most at home with who he was created to be. *Man was created to praise God!*

WORSHIP IS AN ALLEGIANCE

A final word on "Worship—a Christian's Response" is in regard to allegiance. Praise is a form of allegiance, and allegiance is loyalty. Praise is a token of our loyalty. In America, we say the Pledge of Allegiance, which is a statement of our loyalty to the United States of America. It is quoted, predominantly, in schools in America to train children the importance of loyalty to the state. Allegiance simply means to be faithful to or loyal to.

When we praise God—reflecting on His character, His mighty deeds, and His attributes—we are pledging our allegiance to Him. He is the one we will serve. He is the one we will obey. He is the one for whom we lay down our lives. We should ask ourselves where or with whom our allegiance abides? Today we can put our confidence in God, submit our will and plans to Him, and avow our complete allegiance to Him.

Endnotes

[103] Kittel, s.v. "charis."

[104] See Judg. 16:24; 2 Sam. 14:25; 1 Chron. 16:4, 36; 35:5, 30; 25:3; 29:13; 2 Chron. 5:13; 7:6; 8:14; 20:19, 21; 23:12; 30:21; 31:2; Ezra 3:10, 11; Neh. 5:13; 12:24; Ps. 22:22, 23, 26; 35:18; 56:4, 10; 63:5; 69:30, 34; 74:21; 84:4; 102:18; 104:35; 107:32; 109:30; 113:1; 115:17; 115:18; 117:1; 119:164, 175; 135:1, 3; 145:2; 146:1, 2: 147:12; 148:1, 2, 3, 4, 5, 7; 149:3; 150:1,2,3,4,5,6; Ps. 27:2; 31:28; 31:31; Song 6:9; Isa. 62:9; 64:11; Jer. 20:13; 31:7; Joel 2:26.

[105] See Ex. 15:11; Deut. 10:21; 26:19; 1 Chron. 16:35; 2 Chron. 20:22; Neh. 9:5; 12:46; Ps. 9:14; 22:3, 25; 33:1; 34:1; 35:28; 40:3; 48:10; 51:15; 65:1; 66:2, 8; 71:6, 8, 14; 78:4; 79:13; 100:4; 102:21; 106:12, 47: 109:1; 111:10; 119:171; 145:21; 147:1; 148:14; 149:1; Is. 42:8, 10, 12; 43:21; 48:9; 60:6, 18; 61:3, 11: 62:7; 63:7; Jer. 13:11; 17:14; 33:9; 48:2; 49:25; 51:41; Hab. 3:3; Zeph. 3:19, 20.

[106] James Strong, *Strong's Exhaustive Concordance of the Bible* (McLean, VA: Macdonald Publishing, 1993), s.v. "halal."

[107] R. Laird Harris, Gleason Archer, Jr. and Bruce Waltke, *Theological Wordbook of the Old Testament* (Chicago: Moody, 1980), s.v. "halal."

[108] Ibid.

[109] Ibid.

[110] BAGD, s.v. "eulogia."

[111] Kittel, s.v. "aineo."

[112] BAGD, s.v. "epaineo," "epainos." Also see 1 Cor. 11:2, 17, 22.

[113] Vine, s.v. "humneo."

[114] Grudem, chapters 12 & 13.

[115] Grudem, 197.

[116] John 15:13.

[117] Strong, s.v. "doxa."

chapter 10

THE CHURCH—
A Christian's Family

The Church is everywhere represented as one. It is one body, one family, one fold, one kingdom. It is one because [it is] pervaded by one Spirit. We are all baptized into one Spirit so as to become, says the apostle, one body.[118]

—Charles Hodge

The blood of the martyrs is the seed of the church.[119]

—Tertullian

Coming to know Christ is the most important decision we will ever make in life. After that would probably be the finding of a church to call our own. According to the Scriptures, we cannot do without the church: "Not forsaking the assembling of ourselves together, as *is* the manner of some, but exhorting *one another,* and so much the more as you see the Day approaching" (Heb. 10:25 NKIV). Yet, while the church has been the foundation and bedrock of so many communities and cultures throughout the centuries, it has sometimes been the source of much discouragement and control.

Several years ago, I was on a missionary trip to South America, helping a local congregation build a structure that would be suitable for worship. One day we left our work site and were taken to an Amerindian village which was situated on the banks of a deep flowing, but narrow, river. We were warned not to be traveling on the river late in the evening, as we could get lost or have an accident. Well, sure enough, we ended traveling the river in the dark with only a little flashlight to guide the boat. Thankfully, we arrived at the Indian reservation, though late in the night, after traveling ninety miles in a wooden boat. Those of us from America felt like we had navigated to the end of civilization and then taken a left turn. We were cut off from all modern comforts—telephones, electricity, television, and the like.

We stepped out of the boat and planted our feet on the sandy banks of that little river, surveying the landscape of the Indian reservation for the first time. It was a clear, moonlit night, and, to our surprise, one of the first things we noticed was a building with a tin roof glistening in the moonlight. The building was a church. Realizing what the structure was, I was deeply moved. Here, the furthest away from civilization I had ever been, the Gospel had gone before me and had reached this little village. The next day we visited with the wonderful people in that village and heard their story of how this church came to be.

A minister from the city had come to the village a few

years before to preach the Gospel. When he arrived, he found the area in a deplorable state, with many of its people addicted to alcohol (local rum) and living in extreme poverty. This minister told us that he preached the Gospel there and baptized two hundred converts. Later, a group from America came and helped the local villagers build a building. One of the men of the village, who had been addicted to alcohol and had not been providing for his family, became a Christian and returned to being a father and provider for his family. It was this man who eventually became the pastor of that local church. The power of the Gospel transformed that entire place. This church that had caught our eye, as its tin roof glistened in the moonlight, was more than a mere building. It represented the changed lives that resided in the village—it was the Church of the Living God.

WHAT IS THE CHURCH?

The church is not just a building made of brick and mortar. The church is not just an organization that has tax-exempt status with the government. The church is a living, breathing *body* made up of individuals like you and me. It is composed of people who are born again. The Greek term used for church in the New Testament is *ekklesia*, and its most basic definition is "assembly"— implying a calling together of representatives from the ancient Greek cities.[120] In the New Testament, it refers to the assembly of the *called out ones*. The *called out ones* are those who have been washed in the blood of Jesus. This is beautifully portrayed in Acts 20:28 NKJV: "Therefore take heed to yourselves and to all the flock, among which the Holy Spirit has made you overseers, to shepherd the *church* of God which He purchased with His own blood" (emphasis added).

The Protestant Reformers outlined three characteristics of the church—three things that made a church a true church:

- The Proclamation of the Word of God[121]
- The Right Administration of the Sacraments (Ordinances)[122]
- The Faithful Exercise of Church Disciplines

Of course, the Reformers were reacting to the control and domination of the Catholic Church in the sixteenth century. Nevertheless, these insights were profound. In expanding the Reformers' characteristics, we will consider not three but four actions that make a church a *true* church.

God's Word Is Proclaimed

The church must proclaim God's Word.[123] This is why the centerpiece of most Christian worship services is the message that is delivered from the Bible.

> *Those who had been scattered **preached the word wherever** they went. Philip went down to a city in Samaria and proclaimed the Christ there.* (ACTS 8:4-5, EMPHASIS ADDED)

> ***Preach the Word;** be prepared in season and out of season; correct, rebuke and encourage—with great patience and careful instruction.* (2 TIMOTHY 4:2, EMPHASIS ADDED)

Without going into a teaching on correct biblical interpretation, let it suffice that God's Word should be preached *correctly*. In fact, a church that does not preach the Word correctly is not a *true* church. For example, there are thousands of congregations that meet across the world that adhere to an incorrect interpretation of the Scripture and are, in fact, cults. Granted, there should be some liberty in doctrine and some latitude wherein we may disagree with each other. But the interpretation of the Scripture is open to the body of Christ, and we should stand in the great tradition of the historic church. This is why it is important for the church to hold to the ancient creeds.[124]

Where the Where the Ordinances are Observed

The church must observe the ordinances of the Lord's Supper and Baptism.[125] Both of these acts were established by Jesus and the apostles and believers are commanded to practice them throughout every generation.

Baptism. The following Scripture verses emphasize the practice and importance of this ordinance of the church:

> As soon as Jesus was baptized, He went up out of the water. At that moment heaven was opened, and He saw the Spirit of God descending like a dove and lighting on Him. And a voice from heaven said, "This is My Son, whom I love; with Him I am well pleased." (MATTHEW 3:16-17)

> With many other words he warned them; and he pleaded with them, "Save yourselves from this corrupt generation." Those who accepted his message were baptized, and about three thousand were added to their number that day. (ACTS 2:40-41)

The Lord's Supper. Since the Last Supper, which Jesus had with His disciples, the church has practiced, in one form or another, the reenactment of that event. We understand that in the early church the believers would gather together and share a meal. This was called a love meal or *agape* meal. Somewhere in the midst of the meal, the believers would honor the night of Jesus' crucifixion by drinking from the cup and partaking of the bread in honor of His sacrifice.

> While they were eating, Jesus took bread, gave thanks and broke it, and gave it to His disciples, saying, "Take and eat; this is My body." Then He took the cup, gave thanks and offered it to them,

saying, "Drink from it, all of you. This is My blood of the covenant, which is poured out for many for the forgiveness of sins. I tell you, I will not drink of this fruit of the vine from now on until that day when I drink it anew with you in My Father's kingdom." When they had sung a hymn, they went out to the Mount of Olives. (MATTHEW 26:26-30)

Take care, therefore, to participate in one Eucharist (for there is one flesh of our Lord Jesus Christ, and one cup which leads to unity through his blood; there is one altar, just as there is one bishop, together with the presbytery and the deacons, my fellow servants), in order that whatever you do, you do in accordance with God. (The Letter of Ignatius to the Philadelphians, 4).[126]

Where Correction and Accountability Occur

The church is a place where proper discipline takes place.[127] What is meant by this? Firstly, the church is a place of *mutual accountability*—a place where each member should encourage the others to live a life full of God and open to His love and Spirit. This should be a place where each member helps other members who have fallen into sin or trouble.

. . . submitting to one another in the fear of God. (EPHESIANS 5:21 NKJV)

Brothers, if someone is caught in a sin, you who are spiritual should restore him gently. But watch yourself, or you also may be tempted. Carry each other's burdens, and in this way you will fulfill the law of Christ. If anyone thinks he is something when he is nothing, he deceives himself. (GALA-TIANS 6:1-3)

The church is a place where discipline occurs through *the preaching of God's Word.* The Word brings not only comfort and encouragement, but also correction and re-proof. When the Word is preached, the Holy Spirit applies the message to the needs of each person. Second Timothy states this clearly: "All scripture is given by inspiration of God, and is profitable for doctrine, for reproof, for correction, for instruction in righteousness: That the man of God may be perfect, thoroughly furnished unto all good works" (2 Tim. 3:16-17 KJV).

Finally, in regard to correction and accountability, the church is a place where discipline occurs through *the church leadership.* There are many different forms of church government, but every church should have order and structure. In whatever structure exists, God entrusts the power to lead and to discipline with certain individuals. In Matthew 16, Jesus gives His disciples some very powerful instructions related to the power of church leadership:

"On this rock I will build My church, and the gates of Hades shall not prevail against it. And I will give you the keys of the kingdom of heaven, and whatever you bind on earth will be bound in

heaven, and whatever you loose on earth will be loosed in heaven" (MATT. 16:18-19 NKJV).

Where Individuals Find a Place to Serve

The church is a place to serve and to be involved. We often think that the only work that occurs in the church is that of Sunday worship and what the minister or staff are paid to do. However, the church is to be a working body of individuals. It takes every person's gifts and abilities to make this organism, this living entity, thrive and be successful in fulfilling its mission, as Ephesians 4:16 NKJV so aptly expresses, "From whom the whole body, joined and knit together by what every joint supplies, according to the effective working by which every part does its share, causes growth of the body for the edifying of itself in love" (emphasis added).

In making note of the last phrase of this verse—"causes the growth of the body" the thing that causes a church to grow is *the active involvement of the people in the church, using their gifts and abilities.* It is really this simple.

Let us get involved in our local church if we are not already. Let us ask the pastors and other leaders how we can help. When we begin helping in some area, no matter how small or insignificant it may seem, we begin growing in our walk with God. Our growth in our relationship with God involves *doing something* as much as it involves *learning something.* And let us remember that the people we will be working with and worshipping with are human beings just like we are. They have faults and they may sometimes fail, so we must not be discouraged if someone doesn't treat us as we think we should be treated. No one is perfect. And we are not working for the praise and adoration of others anyway. We are working for the church, the kingdom of God, and should desire God's approval more than that of anyone.

WHAT IS THE VISION OF THE CHURCH?

God has a vision for His church. He has a destiny and future for His people. Thus, each local church should have a vision. Whether it is clearly stated or not, most local churches are trying to accomplish something and to be something, realizing all the while that they are part of something larger than themselves. This is all part of what is meant by the vision of the church.

God gives His people vision. Use of the term *vision* in this context is not referring to literal sight with the physical eyes. It has to do with *spiritual* vision. Vision allows for a foretaste of the future. God provides His people with a divine blueprint to guide us into His perfect will for our lives. The Greek term *horao* means *"to see, catch sight of, to notice; to become visible, appear; to experience, witness; to notice, recognize; to be on one's guard."*[128] Seeing denotes perception. It is with the natural eye that we perceive natural things. It is with the spiritual eye that we perceive spiritual things—the things God has prepared for us and the way God wants us to go. This is what vision means when it comes to the church.

Several different terms are translated *vision* in the Bible. Many of them simply refer to seeing with the natural eye. Others deal with divine visions and dreams God gives to His people. Yet, vision, as it applies to our present discussion, is *the perception of the God-specific will for our church and lives.* When we speak of vision for the local church, we are speaking of God's plan and direction for the ministry. We are describing what we feel God wants us to become.

Vision is a powerful tool in the hands of the people of God. Proverbs 29:18 says, "Where there is no revelation [vision], the people cast off restraint." The AMPLIFIED version renders this verse, "Where there is no vision [no redemptive revelations of God], the people perish." Vision is a crucial key to the life and health of a church or *any* organization, for that matter.

In one way or another, every church should be committed to the vision of *seeing lives changed through the power of the Holy Spirit.* Each has a distinct calling to be a church of the Holy Spirit—that is, one that believes in and operates in the fullness of the Holy Spirit's power. It is only through the power of the Spirit that true transformation can occur. In light of all of this, the church has a commitment to see lives transformed.

Jesus' mission and example of ministry should be the church's mission and example to follow. In Luke 4:18-19, we see Jesus' ministry described: "The Spirit of the Lord is on Me, because He has anointed Me to preach good news to the poor. He has sent Me to proclaim freedom for the prisoners and recovery of sight for the blind, to release the oppressed, to proclaim the year of the Lord's favor."

We could say that the church is committed to the *Jesus-style* of ministry—that is, ministering to the *whole* person. With this in mind, we will give attention to five areas of vision that point toward the overall vision of *transforming lives through the power of the Holy Spirit.* I use the term "center" in the following points to show that the local church should be the birthing center for these activities and from there the church should spread out into the local community and into the world. Remember though, when I use the term *church* I am not referring to a physical building but to a living body of believers.

A Center of Worship

Worship is our calling as believers. We were created to worship God. Therefore, the church should be committed to being a center of worship. Worship is about entering into the presence of God. The church should strive to be Spirit-led, not performance driven. The anointing of God is the only thing that breaks through to a person's deepest hurts and needs. The anointing of God rests upon a congregation through authentic praise.

A Center of Discipleship

Jesus gave His disciples the command, "Go and make disciples of all nations, baptizing them in the name of the Father and of the Son, and of the Holy Spirit, and teaching them to obey everything I have commanded you" (Matt. 28:19-20). The emphasis on "making disciples" is extremely important. A disciple is one who follows Jesus and is able, in turn, to lead others in following Him. A disciple reproduces himself. The church should be committed to training disciples of Christ and should be a center of discipleship. Whether they are young or old, everyone has a place in the kingdom of God and can make a positive impact for God.

A Center of Healing

The church must recover its calling to be a healing center. In the day and age in which we live, many lives are fractured and broken. The church needs to rise up and take its rightful place as a healing community—offering spiritual, physical, and emotional healing. The early church was effectively involved in the healing ministry, and this needs to be recovered today.[129] Thank God that many churches are recovering this distinctive by sending out teams on the streets to do healing evangelism. Other churches are hosting healing rooms. Others are training up a new generation to minister healing to the physically and emotionally hurting.

A Center of Community Development

The church is not called to minister only to those within the four walls of its physical building. It has a distinct calling to reach the broader community in which it is situated and then beyond. The church can, and should be, involved in community development. What is meant by this? The church has a unique opportunity in society to be the place where true restoration occurs in the lives of men, women, and children. And it should, for example, take advantage of its position and help transform society by bringing restored people into the workplace, by even assisting its members in establishing businesses that better the community. The church can be involved in helping immigrants assimilate the culture and language of the community. It can assist youth and children in their studies, even provide schools, colleges, universities, after-school tutoring, home schooling networks, and so on.

As many already know, the church has been active in helping the poor and downtrodden in society. It *should* be involved in distributing food and clothing to the needy. It *should* be involved in bringing the Good News to those who are incarcerated. It has a golden opportunity to help in all kinds of ways those who are needy in many respects. Tommy Barnett, a leading pastor in America in the Assemblies of God, once said, "If you minister to people's needs, you'll never lack a crowd."

A Center of Church Extension

One final point is worth mentioning in regard to the vision of the church. The church must reproduce itself and have in mind just how it will do this. What if every church in America planted a sister congregation, one like its own, in another community? It doesn't take a rocket scientist to figure out that the number of churches in America would double. Research has shown that new churches are the most effective in growing and reaching the community. So, let us consider that we would have twice the number of churches and be more effective in reaching communities for Christ if each church would commit to *mothering* just one other church.

Let us take this a step further and ask, "What if every church in America planted a new congregation in an area of need—as in an inner city or poverty-stricken community—in their city or state?" If this would happen, the amount of support and transformation these communities would receive would be incalculable.

Finally, what if every local church in America planted a new congregation in a foreign country? How many unreached people could we reach? This would dramatically revolutionize world missions.

In essence, every church needs to think about how it can reproduce and reach other communities and nations. The church exists to reproduce itself.

WHAT ARE THE CORPORATE VALUES OF A CHURCH?

Most corporations have a set of values that determines how the corporation will operate. Values have been defined, in a corporate sense, as ". . . traits or qualities that are considered worthwhile; they represent . . . [the] highest priorities and deeply held driving forces."[130] It is good to define the corporate values of a local church, just as it is good to define the values of one's individual life. To follow is a list of some possible values for governing the church. These were applied in a church planting in which I was involved in the greater Washington, D.C., metropolitan area. These values, applied in this particular situation, are being shared only as an example and as *possible* guidelines. Another church may have a different set of values. Other church leaders or planters could use these as a pattern for those that they, along with their leadership team, will craft for their particular situation.

Christ the Head

Jesus Christ is the head of the church and we are to submit ourselves to His will and purposes. Ephesians 1:22-23 tells us, "And God placed all things under His feet and appointed Him to be head over everything for the church, which is His body, the fullness of Him who fills everything in every way."

Prayer

Prayer is our lifeline to God in the conception, planning, and execution of all ministries.

> *"Ask and it will be given to you; seek and you will find; knock and the door will be opened to you. For everyone who asks receives; he who seeks finds; and to him who knocks, the door will be opened. Which of you, if his son asks for bread, will give him a stone? Or if he asks for a fish, will give him a snake? If you, then, though you are evil, know how to give good gifts to your children, how much more will your Father in heaven give good gifts to those who ask him!"* (MATTHEW 7:7-11)

Children

We value children and are committed to training them up to be Christ-like. In Deuteronomy 6:6-7, we read, "These commandments that I give you today are to be upon your hearts. Impress them on your children. Talk about them when you sit at home and when you walk along the road, when you lie down and when you get up."

Worship

We are committed to exalting the Lord Jesus Christ in authentic worship. In John 4:23-24, Jesus Himself tells us, "Yet a time is coming and has now come when the true worshipers will worship the Father in spirit and truth, for they are the kind of worshipers the Father seeks. God is spirit, and His worshipers must worship in spirit and in truth."

Lost

We value people and will use whatever God-honoring means are available to win them to Christ. Again, it is Jesus who says, "It is not the healthy who need a doctor, but the sick" (Matt. 9:12).

Spiritual Maturity

We desire to bring believers into a mature relationship with Jesus Christ through relevant biblical preaching and teaching. "All Scripture is God-breathed and is useful for teaching, rebuking, correcting and training in righteousness" (2 Tim. 3:16).

Relationships

We are committed to strengthening relationships through small groups where people may reach the lost, exercise their spiritual gifts, be nurtured, and mature in Christ's likeness. In Acts 2:44-46, we see that the New Testament church set the pace for this: "All the believers were together and had everything in common. Selling their possessions and goods, they gave to anyone as he had need. Every day they continued to meet together in the temple courts. They broke bread in their homes and ate together with glad and sincere hearts" (Acts 2:44-46).

Leadership

We value godly and transparent leadership that exists to develop and release others into their calling, just as Paul desired to do, as is recorded in the following Scripture verse: "And the things you have heard me say in the presence of many witnesses entrust to reliable men who will also be qualified to teach others" (2 Tim. 2:2).

Church Planting

We are committed to being a church that plants other churches in the United States and in foreign countries. This is in accordance with what Acts 1:8 admonishes us to do: "But you will receive power when the Holy Spirit comes on you; and you will be My witnesses in Jerusalem, and in all Judea and Samaria, and to the ends of the earth."

Missions

We are committed to being missions minded. We will adopt unreached people groups and partner with others to see church planting movements established among these. We take very seriously the words of Matthew 24:14, which read, "And this gospel of the kingdom will be preached in the whole world as a testimony to all nations, and then the end will come."

Excellence

Since God gave His best in Christ, we value excellence in all our activities and ministries. In Colossians 3:23-24, Paul admonishes this very thing: "Whatever you do, work at it with all your heart, as working for the Lord, not for men, since you know that you will receive an inheritance from the Lord as a reward. It is the Lord Christ you are serving."

WHAT IS THE MISSION OF THE CHURCH?

Mission is simply the practical side of the vision. The vision tells *what* we believe God wants us to become, whereas the mission tells *how* we believe we are going to achieve what God wants us to become. The mission fulfills the vision. Below is a simple illustration of a cross that will help us memorize four points of the church's mission.

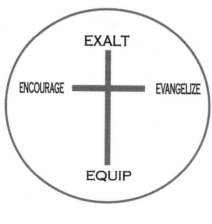

The top of the vertical line reminds us of our first duty—to worship God. The opposite end of the vertical line reminds us of our duty to ground ourselves in the Word of God—to be properly equipped. The horizontal line reminds us of our mission—to humanity. Firstly, we must evangelize the lost; secondly, we must encourage our fellow believers. This simple paradigm encapsulates the four points of the church's mission:

- Exalt God in worship
- Encourage fellow believers.
- Equip believers through the Word
- Evangelize the lost

We have looked at the characteristics, vision, values, and mission of the church. Jesus said the gates of hell would not prevail against it. (Matt. 16:18.) Throughout its history, governments and individuals have tried to stop it. Yet, the church remains. In times of persecution and hardship, it endures. It even grows through the tough times. We must not lose heart and be an active part of the local church.

Endnotes

[118] Charles Hodge, What is Presbyterianism? An address delivered before the Presbyterian Historical Society at their anniversary meeting, on Tuesday evening, May 1, 1855.

[119] Tertullian Apologeticum 50 [http://www.tertullian.

[120] Kittel, s.v. "ekklesia."

[121] Robert Reymond, *A New Systematic Theology of the Christian Faith* (Nashville; Nelson, 1998), 868f. org/works/apologeticum.htm]. Accessed 2013.

[122] In this work I will use the term *ordinance* to avoid confusion with *sacramental theology* (which states that grace is conveyed through the sacraments). Yet, it should be noted that some Protestant groups use the term *sacrament,* as did the Protestant Reformers, to refer to these acts commanded by Christ. *Ordinance* indicates that these acts were *ordained* or *commanded* by Christ to be observed by his followers.

[123] Also see John 8:31, 47; 14:23; Gal. 1:8-9; 2 Thess. 2:15; 2 Tim. 3:16-4:4; 1 John 4:1-3; 2 John 9-11.

[124] Leith, see Nicean Creed 28-31, Constantinopolitan Creed 31-33, Definition of Chalcedon 34-36.

[125] Also see 1 Cor. 10:14-21; 11:23-30.

[126] Michael W. Holmes, ed., *The Apostolic Fathers* (Grand Rapids: Baker, 1999).

[127] Also see Matt. 18:17; Acts 20:28-31; Rom. 16:17-18; 1 Cor. 5:1-5; 14:33, 40; Eph. 5:6,11; 2 Thess. 3:14-15; 1 Tim. 1:20; 5:20; Titus 1:10-11; 3:10; Rev. 2:14-16; 2:20.

[128] BAGD, s.v. "orao."

[129] On this point, I would like to refer the reader to Francis MacNutt, *The Healing Reawakening* (Grand Rapids: Chosen, 2005). The book traces the history of the healing ministry, how it was lost, and how the contemporary church has recovered it. In light of its thesis, the book was initially titled, *The Nearly Perfect Crime.*

[130] Susan M. Heathfield, "Build a Strategic Framework: Mission

Statement, Vision, Values" [http://humanresources.about.com/cs/strategicplanning1/a/strategicplan_3.htm], Accessed September 2012.

EPILOGUE

Eugene Peterson defined Christian discipleship as "a long obedience in the same direction."[131] Living the Christian life is a lifetime journey. We are spoiled, in the contemporary world, by technology that has allowed things to come to us instantly. Fast food, microwave cooking, online news sites, social media, and the like, are all commonplace in today's society. Yet, there are no shortcuts to a deep relationship with God. It takes days, months, and years to develop a deep relationship with God. This is one of the beauties of Christianity. As you continue to walk with the Lord, the relationship will deepen. Your understanding will deepen. Your prayer life will deepen. Your relationships with other believers will deepen.

So, enjoy the journey! Put to use the things you have read in this book. Develop a regular time with God. Get into His Word and let it speak to you. Go to the Father in prayer and learn to commune with Him. You're not too young, and you're not too old. Now is you're time to walk with God. Pursue Him!

Endnote

[131] Eugene Peterson, *A Long Obedience in the Same Direction* (Downer's Gove: InterVarsity Press, 2000).

WORKS CITED

Works Cited

The American Heritage Dictionary, Second Ed. Boston: Houghton Mifflin, 1985.

Anselm of Canterbury. *The Major Works of Anselm of Canterbury*, eds. Brian Davies and G.R. Evans. London: Oxford Press, 1998.

Aquinas, Thomas. *The Summa Theologica of St. Thomas Aquinas*, Second and Revised Edition, 1920. Literally translated by Fathers of the English Dominican Province.

Augustine. *Confessions*. Trans. Rex Warner. New York: Penguin, 1963.

------. *City of God*. Trans. Henry Bettensen. New York: Penguin, 2003.

Barrett, David. *World Christian Encyclopedia: A Comparative Survey of Churches and Religions in the Modern World.* London: Oxford University Press, 2001.

Bauer, Walter; William F. Arndt; and F. Wilbur Ginrich. *A Greek-English Lexicon of the New Testament and Other Christian Literature.* Chicago: University of Chicago Press, 1979.

Bennett, Dennis. *How to Pray for the Release of the Holy Spirit.* South Plainfield: Bridge, 1985.

Bright, Bill. *The Coming Revival: America's Call to Fast, Pray, and "Seek God's Face."* Orlando: New Life, 1995.

------. *Witnessing Without Fear.* Nashville: Thomas Nelson, 1986.

The New Brown-Driver-Briggs-Gesenius Hebrew and English Lexicon. Peabody, MA.: Hendrickson, 1979.

Burlingame, Michael, ed. *Lincoln Observed: The Civil War Dispatches of Noah Brooks.* Baltimore: Johns Hopkins University Press, 1998.

Calvin, John. *Institutes of the Christian Religion.* Trans. Henry Beveridge. Grand Rapids: Zondervan, 1995.

Camus, Albert. *The Myth of Sisyphus*. Trans. Justin O'Brien. New York: Alfred A. Knopf, Inc., 1955.

Carson, D.A. *Gospel of Matthew*. Grand Rapids: Zondervan, 1984.

Colson, Charles W. *Loving God* (Grand Rapids: Zondervan, 1983), 131.

Comfort, Ray and Kirk Cameron. *Way of the Master.* North Brunswick, NJ: Bridge-Logos, 2006.

The Constitution of the United Presbyterian Church in the United States of America: Part 1, Book of Confession. Philadelphia, PA: The General Assembly of the United Presbyterian Church in the United States of America, 1967.

Erickson, Millard. *Christian Theology*. Baker: Grand Rapids, 1985.

------. *Readings in Christian Theology: The New Life.* Vol. 3, ed. Millard J. Erickson. Grand Rapids: Baker, 1979.

Fisher, Mary Pat. *Living Religions*. Upper Saddle River, NJ: Prentice Hall, 2002.

Geisler, Norman and Peter Bochino. *Unshakable Foundations: Contemporary Answers to Crucial Questions About the Christian Faith*. Minneapolis: Bethany, 2001.

Gerhard Kittel and Gerhard Friedrich, eds. *Theological Dictionary of the New Testament.* Grand Rapids: Eerdmans, 1985.

Gilbert, Josiah Hotchkiss. *Dictionary of Burning Words of Brilliant Writers.* Whitefish, MT: Kessinger Publishing, LLC, 2009.

Graves, Robert W. *Praying in the Spirit.* Old Tappen: Chosen, 1987.

Green, Michael. *But Don't All Religions Lead to God?* Grand Rapids: Baker, 2002.

Gregory of Nyssa, Orat. *Catech.* PG.

Grudem, Wayne. *Systematic Theology.* Grand Rapids: Zondervan, 1994.

Hagin, Kenneth. *Welcome to God's Family.* Tulsa: Faith Publications, 1997.

Hall, T. William, ed. *Introduction to the Study of Religion.* San Francisco: Harper and Row, 1978.

R. Laird Harris, Gleason Archer, Jr. and Bruce Waltke. *Theological Wordbook of the Old Testament.* Chicago: Moody, 1980.

Hathfield, Susan M. "Build a Strategic Framework: Mission Statement, Vision, Values." http://humansresources.about.com/cs/strategiplanning1/a/strategicplan_3.html.

Heflin Jr., Wallace. *The Power of Prophecy.* Hagerstown: McDougal, 1995.

Hinn, Benny. *Good Morning Holy Spirit.* Nashville: Nelson, 1990.

Hodge, Charles. *Systematic Theology*, Abridged Edition. Grand Rapids: Baker, 1992.

Holmes, Michael W., ed. *The Apostolic Fathers.* Grand Rapids: Baker, 1999.

Hybels, Bill and Mittleburg, Mark. *Becoming a Contagious Christian.* Grand Rapids: Zondervan, 1996.

Kierkegaard, Soren. *The Journals of Søren Kierkegaard*, trans., ed. Alexander Dru. London: Oxford University Press, 1938.

------. *Parables of Kierkegaard*, ed. Thomas Oden. Princeton: Princeton University Press, 1978.

Leith, John H., ed. *Creeds of the Churches.* Louisville: John Knox Press, 1963.

Lewis, C.S., *Mere Christianity.* New York: Macmillan, 1952.

------. *Letters to Malcolm: Chiefly on Prayer.* New York: Harcourt, Inc. 2002.

Luther, Martin. *Concordia: The Lutheran Confessions: A Reader's Edition of the Book of Concord*, Smalcald Articles. St. Louis: Concordia, 2005.

MacNutt, Francis. *The Healing Reawakening.* Grand Rapids: Chosen, 2005.

Moore, Peter. *A Step Further: The Journey in Discipleship.* Charlestown: Advantage, 2011.

Müller, George. *Answers to Prayer.* Feather Trail Press, 2010.

Müller George. *Orphanages Built by Prayer.* http://www.christan-ity.com/church/church-history/church-history-for-kids/george-mueller-orphanages-built-by-prayer-11634869.html.

Murry, Andrew. *Humility: The Journey Toward Holiness* (Min-neapolis: Bethany House, 2001) Chapter 7.

Navigators. "Thirty Days of Praying the Names and Attributes of God." Colorado Springs, CO: www.navigators.org, 2012.

Olson, Roger E. *The Story of Christian Theology: Twenty Centuries of Tradition and Reform.* Downers Grover: Inter Varsity Press, 1999.

O'Sullivan, John. *The President, the Pope, and the Prime Minister: Three Who Changed the World.* Washington D.C.: Regnery, 2005.

Osborn, T.L. *Healing & God's Will.* [http://jesus-is-lord.alberta-rose.org/TLOsborn.htm].

Page, Kirby. *Living Abundantly.* New York: Farrar & Rinehart, Incor-porated, 1944.

Pannenberg, Wolfhart. *Systematic Theology*, vol. 1. Grand Rapids: Eerdmans, 1991.

------. *Systematic Theology*, vol. 2. Grand Rapids: Zondervan, 1994.

Peterson, Eugene. *A Long Obedience in the Same Direction.* Downer's Gove: InterVarsity Press, 2000.

Pike, Garnet. *Receiving the Promise of the Father: How To Be Baptized in the Holy Spirit.* Franklin Springs: Lifesprings Resources, 2000.

Piper, John. *Let the Nations Be Glad! The Supremacy of God in Missions,* Second Edition. Grand Rapids: Baker, 1993.

Reymond, Robert. *A New Systematic Theology of the Christian Faith.* Nashville: Nelson, 1998.

Schaeffer, Francis. *He Is There and He Is Not Silent.* Wheaton: Tyndale, 2001.

Slick, Matt. "Why believe in Christianity over all other religions?"

[http://carm.org/why-believe-christianity-over-all-other-religions].

Smith, Huston. *The World's Religions.* San Francisco: Harper, 1991. James Strong. *Strong's Exhaustive Concordance of the Bible.* McLean, VA: Macdonald Publishing, 1993.

Thieleke, Helmut. *Modern Faith and Thought.* Grand Rapids: Eerdmans, 1990.

Synan, Vinson. *The Holiness-Pentecostal Movement in the United States.* Grand Rapids: Eerdmans, 1971.

Underwood, B.E., *Spiritual Gifts: Ministries and Manifestations.* Franklin Springs: Lifesprings, 1984.

W.E. Vine, *Vine's Expository Dictionary of New Testament Words,* unabridged ed. (McClean, VA: MacDonald Pub-lishing, 1989

Voltaire. *Voltaire in His Letters,* trans. S.G. Tallentyre. Honolulu: University Press of the Pacific, 1919.

Wagner, C. Peter. *Strategies for Church Growth.* Ventura: Regal, 1989.

Wesley, John. "Letter to Alexander Mather on August 6, 1777." The Wesley Center online, [http://wesley.nnu.edu/john-wesley/the-letters-of-john-wesley/wesleys-letters-1777].

------. Journal entry May 24, 1738. [http://www.ccel.org/ccel/wesley/journal.vi.ii.xvi.html].

Williams, J. Rodman. *Renewal Theology,* vol. 1-2. Grand Rapids: Zondervan, 1988.

Williams, Pat. *How to Be Like Jesus: Lessons in Following in His Footsteps.* Deerfield Beach, FL.: Health Com-munications, 2003.

Wurmbrand, Richard. *Tortured for Christ.* Glendale, CA: Diane Books, 1967.

Zacharias, Ravi. *Can Man Live Without God?* Waco: Word, 1994.